Praise for *Clutter Busting Your Life*

"Clutter is so much more than the physical objects we cling to. Fortunately, Brooks Palmer is so much more than a clutter buster. The defenses, anger, and general dopiness we use to protect our tender selves are no match for his gentleness, humor, and insight. Through compelling stories and simple exercises he helps us identify and release our attachment to the stuff that's getting in the way of our happiness. I'm beginning to think that Brooks might be able to clutter bust us all the way to world peace."

— Colleen Wainwright, writer, speaker, and creator of Communicatrix.com

"*Clutter busting* is a clever and useful term for eliminating everything in your life that does not serve you, including certain persons and relationship patterns. *Clutter Busting Your Life* is filled with interesting stories and useful guidance about replacing physical and emotional baggage with freedom and joyful relationships."

— Harville Hendrix, PhD, author of *Getting the Love You Want: A Guide for Couples*

"Both physical and emotional clutter can take up a lot of space. In *Clutter Busting Your Life*, Brooks Palmer provides inspiring examples, humor, and encouragement to help readers let go of clutter, along with small steps that can help people create a new and joyful life. If you're looking for ways to let go of clutter, then this book is for you."

— Tammy Strobel, author of *You Can Buy Happiness (and It's Cheap)* and RowdyKittens.com

Praise for *Clutter Busting*

"*Clutter Busting* literally changed my life. Brooks's gentle yet firm voice inspired me to act, to widen my eyes and take a fresh look around — and undo pockets of clutter, not only in my closet and the trunk of my car but also in my heart. This book is filled with practical, useful wisdom."

— Marc Lesser, author of
Less: Accomplishing More by Doing Less

"I have needed this book for years, and I loved it! Brooks's advice helped me clean up clutter, which gave me more time, energy, and creativity."

— Robert J. Kriegel, PhD, *New York Times* bestselling
author of *If It Ain't Broke, Break It!*

"If you want to make your space into a transformative tool that supports your life and work, you need *Clutter Busting*."

— Julia Mossbridge, PhD, author of
Unfolding: The Perpetual Science of Your Soul's Work

"Before I even finished this book, I had to start implementing some of the recommendations. By the time I read the last page, not only my home but also my family dynamic and my career were unrecognizable. It was like a miracle."

— Debra Halperin Poneman, founder of Yes to Success
Seminars and bestselling author of
Chicken Soup for the American Idol Soul

CLUTTER
BUSTING
YOUR LIFE

CLUTTER BUSTING
YOUR LIFE

Clearing Physical and
Emotional Clutter to Reconnect
with Yourself and Others

BROOKS PALMER

New World Library
Novato, California

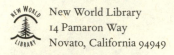

New World Library
14 Pamaron Way
Novato, California 94949

The material in this book is intended for educational purposes only. No expressed or implied guarantee as to the effects of the use of the recommendations can be given nor liability taken.

Text design by Tona Pearce Myers

Library of Congress Cataloging-in-Publication Data
Palmer, Brooks, date.
 Clutter busting your life : clearing physical and emotional clutter to reconnect with yourself and others / Brooks Palmer.
     p.   cm.
ISBN 978-1-60868-079-5 (pbk. : alk. paper)
1. Self-actualization (Psychology) 2. Interpersonal relations. I. Title.
BF637.S4.P35 2012
158—dc23   2012006065

First printing, May 2012
ISBN 978-1-60868-079-5
Printed in the USA on 100% postconsumer-waste recycled paper

New World Library is proud to be a Gold Certified Environmentally Responsible Publisher. Publisher certification awarded by Green Press Initiative. www.greenpressinitiative.org

10 9 8 7 6 5 4 3 2 1

This book is dedicated to you. Thank you for being open to letting go of your false armor. Our hearts are more powerful than anything we hide behind to protect ourselves.

The store was closed so I went home and hugged what I own.

CONTENTS

INTRODUCTION

I never set out to write another clutter-busting book. When I finished my first book, *Clutter Busting: Letting Go of What's Holding You Back*, I felt I had covered all the bases for every type of clutter. I meant it to be truly an all-purpose clutter book, the only one you'd ever need. The gist of my message was: You are sacred. Your stuff is not. In that book I made clear that clutter is anything in your life that no longer serves you, and that when you get rid of that clutter, you feel better.

Then I went on a book tour around the country to promote *Clutter Busting*, and at every gathering people asked me questions about relationships. They understood how to deal with the clutter in their homes and offices, but they still had questions about clutter in terms of their relationships with others — family members, partners, colleagues, and friends.

A common question was "What should I say to my

1

brother (or sister or friend or husband)? I hate going to his house. He has stuff all over the place. I want him to get rid of things, so what should I say so that he'll do it?"

I'd answer, "Nothing. There's nothing you can do. You can't make somebody do something. I can't clutter bust someone in their home if they're not open to it, and you can't either."

People seemed let down by that answer. I started to see that often another person's clutter becomes clutter for the person bothered by it. This dynamic extends to many situations. There is clutter within people's relationships with others. Some people brought up the gifts they'd received: "So-and-so gave me this thing and I don't like it, but I can't get rid of it." They feared that getting rid of the unwanted gift would upset the person or somehow be disrespectful of their relationship. That fear in itself became clutter because it interfered with the relationship between the recipient of the gift and the giver.

Sometimes someone would bring a partner, friend, or family member to the talk and then "out" his or her cluttery ways, expecting me to tell this person that they should get rid of their stuff. This often made them defensive, and an argument would ensue. It made things worse.

Other people talked about furniture and other artifacts they'd inherited from a deceased relative. They felt oppressed by this stuff but also tremendously guilty for even thinking about clutter busting the deceased's belongings.

In all these situations, it became clear that the question of what to keep and what to throw away was more complicated and nuanced than just evaluating one's own opinion about an item. The real clutter was frequently people's conflicted emotions about someone else. They wanted to know how to get some relief.

What was going on was subtler than the question posed in my first book: "Do you love this, or can you let it go?"

The purpose of that question was to help my readers determine whether something was part of their life or not. Asking this question is a way to be direct and honest with yourself: to consider something — a tangible object, a person, a situation, or a way of living — and asking whether or not it is really part of your life right now. There's something clarifying about honestly considering an item and seeing how you feel about it. That is the crux of clutter busting.

This book, *Clutter Busting Your Life*, delves more deeply into the nature of our *relationships* — our connections with ourselves and with the people in our lives — and how clutter intrudes, distorts, and diminishes these connections. The intrusion itself becomes clutter. This book illuminates what happens when we become emotionally involved in relationship clutter and lose sight of the connection and joy that come from the relationship itself. This subtle awareness allows the interference of clutter to diminish so that we can enjoy the relationship again. Clearing this internal clutter is even more profound than getting rid of our things because our greatest joy comes from our connection with ourselves and others. In sum, anything that interferes with, blocks, interrupts, or destroys this joy is clutter.

How This Book Is Organized

The main purpose of clutter busting is to reconnect with ourselves. When we are mentally or emotionally divorced from ourselves, we suffer. What I've learned from my more than ten years as a professional clutter buster is that we often embody this disconnection in our homes and workplaces: those piles of moldy boxes, those counters and desks covered with stacks of paper, that couch we hate but can't seem to part with, the overstuffed clothes closet, the storage locker we've been afraid to revisit for three years, the densely packed and tangled drawers and cabinets — all represent some cluttered aspect of our inner life.

So the first relationship I address in this book is the one we have with ourselves. Having a deeper understanding of this relationship makes it easier to understand our relationships with others. This book starts by shining a spotlight on the things in our lives that affect our relationship with ourselves. We look at what we bring into our lives in an attempt to cover up our innate lovingness. Things that make us smarter, more beautiful, more powerful, more spiritual, or more prosperous are not bad in and of themselves, but when we use them as armor for our gentle selves, we end up losing the connection with the part of ourselves that is crucial for our peace of mind and happiness. This dynamic is also fundamental in our relationships with others.

Once we have shined a spotlight on ourselves, we review basic clutter-busting techniques. Even for those who have read the first book, this review contains important reminders of what the process entails and how to approach it. The rest of the book then takes you through all aspects of clutter busting within your relationships.

The first step is to look at how we use clutter as a buffer against others. We try to defend ourselves from being hurt in relationships by protecting ourselves with stuff. What we really want is to feel safe and connected with others, but this armor destroys the experience of unity that we crave. Clutter shields provide us with a sense of power, but it is a false power; our defenses only increase our disconnection. Our fear, pain, and grief hypnotize us into believing we need these shields to avoid more hurt, but we don't. In fact, we are stronger without them. No amount of armor can give us peace of mind. I know because I've tried, and so have all my clients.

Then we consider the ways in which relationships are tangible things. Often we think of relationships as abstract. We diminish them in our minds. In the same way that space exists in a room but is covered up by the things in that space, our relationships exist but are obscured by emotional clutter. Relationships need our attention as much as our bodies, cars, and homes.

One of the main ways this emotional clutter manifests is in our attempts to control others so they won't hurt us. Unfortunately, these efforts create distance, dispelling connection and concealing the delicate feelings of closeness and spontaneity that bring us joy. The clutter of control creates suffering.

We'll also take a look at how we unknowingly hide our emotional or relationship clutter in our living spaces. This clutter was too much to bear, and so we hid it under our stuff. When we begin to clutter bust, it comes to the surface of our awareness. Because we have a lot of unresolved feelings to process, we can get overwhelmed and take it out on the person we share the space with. In this book I suggest some gentler ways to ride through this storm so that healing can take place.

Then we'll investigate how past relationships can negatively influence us, particularly those with former romantic partners, with ex-friends, and with deceased parents and relatives. Our emotional attachments can keep painful aspects of these relationships alive and prevent us from moving on or from starting new, healthy relationships. When we take a closer look, we see how clutter keeps us tied to the past. Seeing this allows us to break through the restrictive aspects of that bond while maintaining the connections with the people we love.

When we investigate the clutter in our relationships, we sometimes find that someone in our lives has themselves become clutter. Perhaps they weren't originally, but our current relationship with them is now harming us, and we don't see it because of our attachment to positive memories. Sometimes relationships were never healthy to begin with. Just like our things, a relationship is clutter when it doesn't serve our well-being. So we'll examine when it's okay to clutter bust a person.

In the last chapter, I talk about how to clutter bust with someone else. You can clutter bust successfully with a partner, friend, family member, or coworker. The clutter-busting process itself can become a way to build and reinforce kind and honest relationships. For example, I once worked with a couple who were arguing over almost everything I was asking them about. At one point, they were in a particularly heated disagreement over where in their bedroom to put a painting a relative had given them. This painting had been on the floor and leaning against the wall for more than a year. I stepped in and simplified things by asking, "Do you like this painting?" They both answered clearly at the same time, "No." Then they laughed together. That "no" reconnected them. Their argument was actually not about the painting but about their broken connection. By simplifying things, they were able to let go of the involvement with their relationship clutter, reconnect, and work together again without interference. The last chapter will teach you how to do this in your relationships.

Throughout, I provide exercises to help you put all this into practice. Some help you identify your clutter armor and assist you in removing it. This armor wears you out and doesn't look very good on you anyway. Other exercises focus on the emotional clutter that's disturbing you and your relationships. Still others are designed to be done with the people you are close to.

In the end, this book takes the original clutter-busting question, "Is this of actual value to me, or can I get rid of it?" and brings it into a deeper place that reconnects you with yourself and others. We will learn to look matter-of-factly at the things in our environment and determine if they help or hurt our lives and relationships. It might be scary to consider something we're invested in. But what if we're living with something that is actually hurting us?

Connection with another is our most joyful experience, and this book will help you remove any obstacles to it.

No one knew of the buried treasure, so it was worthless.

Chapter One

THE CLUTTER OF FALSE ARMOR

I came to my client's front door and was greeted by a small piece of paper covering the glass. The words on it read, "Occupants are home and are armed." The word *armed* had been heavily underlined with a pen. I thought, "It's the antiwelcome mat. I think he wants to be left alone." It's a good thing I don't take these things personally.

I rang the buzzer. From behind the door I heard a defensive, "Who is it?" I said, "It's Brooks, the clutter-busting guy." I heard the clicks of four door locks opening. The door cracked opened slightly, and a man's face peered out. I nodded and said hi, and he opened the door the rest of the way. The man was in his late fifties and dressed in black and had a tough-guy, don't-mess-with-me air. He reminded me of Charles Bronson in *Death Wish*. I shook his hand, and for a moment I could see fear and sadness in his eyes beneath his rough veneer. I remember thinking that it felt as if his inner core was filled with tears.

My client invited me in. It was difficult to get past the stacks of paper and boxes obscuring the entrance. The space was dark. Some light from a dim bulb at the end of the hallway revealed the pathways he had carved for himself out of the clutter. They were mazes. The musty smell of mold in the air made it difficult to breathe. He boasted that I was only the third person he had let into his house in the past twelve years.

Then he gave me a tour of the house. I couldn't see the extent of the clutter on each floor because the walls of clutter were a couple of feet taller than me. Bungee cords held them back so they wouldn't collapse. I feared the cords would break and the mounds of stuff would topple and kill us both. My client showed me where he slept — on a soiled comforter lying in one of the pathways. The place felt haunted.

There was no empty space. There was no feeling of life in the place. He said in his rough-and-gruff, matter-of-fact voice that every night for the past six months he had lain in bed and put a shotgun in his mouth. But for some reason, he couldn't get himself to pull the trigger.

It was the first time I felt overwhelmed in a job. I didn't know how I could help this client. Then tears began to fill his eyes. He tried clearing his throat to stop the emotions that were erupting. He said in a soft, cracking voice, "I can't take the pain of this anymore. I feel so ashamed that I'm living this way." That was the opening, the crack letting in the light. His pretend wall of toughness had tumbled, revealing his fragility.

I was suddenly inspired. I grabbed a trash bag and waded into the clutter. I said, "Let's start here!" He looked stunned. I pulled out an empty soda bottle. I said, "What about this? Do you need this, or can we let it go?" He didn't know what to say. He was filled with so much inertia that it was hard for him to think. Somehow he managed to say, "I guess I can let it go."

As we worked he told me he used to live clutter-free. He had few possessions, and he liked living with open space. He used to be very social. He worked at a top-level creative job that he loved. His colleagues there felt like his family. But twelve years ago he was fired in an abrupt and unkind manner. My client was deeply hurt, and he reacted defensively by shutting himself off from the world. He filled his home with needless things to insulate himself from the world. But he could never feel safe enough.

After a few hours of working together, I asked him, "How about the sign on your front door, the one that says, 'Occupants are home and are *armed*'? Can we let it go?"

He went dark and tough again, and his vulnerability vanished. He said, "No, that sign stays! I need to protect myself. No one's ever tried to break in because that's up there!"

I gently told him that the sign wasn't protecting him from the one person who was causing him the greatest pain and misery — himself. He made himself live in squalor. Every night he put a shotgun barrel in his mouth and threatened his life. He terrorized himself. The sign wasn't stopping him.

Tears flooded his eyes, and he cried for a while, his whole body shaking. It felt as if shackles were breaking off his body. This man felt the need to protect himself from being hurt with an aura of violence and power. But the things he was using to protect himself hadn't made him safer; they had hurt him. He saw that he couldn't rely on them anymore, and the mighty power of his heart came to his defense. My client went downstairs and took down the sign. When he came back up, the color had returned to his face. I could feel his true presence shining through. It reminded me of the movie *The Exorcist*, when the demon leaves the little girl and she's healthy again.

We spent the next few months dismantling the clutter fortress in his home. As we worked side by side, I could see his inspiration grow as he came home to his heart.

Having dropped his severe protective stance, he reconnected with a girlfriend from thirty years ago, and they became a couple again. He spent evenings and weekends with her, and they relished their time together. By dropping his false armor, he restored his connection with himself, and he became open to connecting with others.

When this remarkable client finished clutter busting, he sold his home and rented a small cottage from some long-lost friends. Now he sees them daily and often has dinner with them. He also took up painting and has been showing his art in galleries in Los Angeles. My client also got a job helping people out of unfortunate and desperate situations. I still keep in contact with him. It seems he found that the only safe and satisfying way to live is being open to his beautiful, innate sensitivity, without the inter-ference of clutter.

The Beauty of Being Sensitive

The dominant factor of all your experiences is your rela-tionship with yourself. When you have a strong connec-tion with your open, sensitive self, you tend to move with the flow of events. You derive greater personal satisfaction from your life. You feel a thriving curiosity about the way things are. You experience greater clarity, seeing things as they are in front of you.

When the clutter in your life cuts you off from experi-encing this basic relationship, when the connection with yourself is weak, you can experience anguish over different aspects of your life. You can experience great worry and fear about possible future events. Your relationships with others are often chaotic. You misinterpret what's happen-ing and make decisions that cause you even more grief.

For more than ten years, I've seen hundreds of people let go of the clutter of false armor they once desperately hung on to in order to feel safe. They replaced living in fear with embracing the beauty of an openly sensitive life.

When I speak of sensitivity, I don't mean this in a negative way. Being sensitive is often equated with being weak. "If I'm open to feeling too much, I can get hurt." I like to use the word *sensitivity* more positively. Being sensi-tive means being aware of ourselves and our environment. We know what we feel. We sense when something feels good, and we know when something hurts. When we are open, we respond in a way that nourishes and protects us. When we deny that, when we cover that up, we are living in numbness. We can't respond positively if we're not aware of what's going on. In a certain sense, we're not protected, even though we think we are.

Naturally, we want to protect ourselves. Some protective measures are useful and make a positive difference in our lives. And then there's clutter. My client tried to protect himself by hiding behind a tough persona and behind walls of stuff. These pseudo-protective devices make us feel safe, but maintaining this armor comes at a cost. We get lost in our efforts to preserve our false armor and don't see that it in-fact hurts us. It keeps us from the joyful connections we most want, and it disrupts the creativity and flexibility we need to live a happy, connected life.

By clutter busting, we identify which of the things in our homes and lives are hurting us so we can let go of them and start feeling connected with ourselves again. When we remove these impediments to connection, we experience joy.

Openness to Intuition

A natural strength comes from being open. We feel the hum of life itself, regardless of whether or not we like what is going on in our lives. When we're open, we naturally tap into our intelligence and intuition.

Like a lot of people, for many years before I went to college I was kind of clueless. I walked around in a trance of anger. On some level I felt the anger served me because it felt like protection; it kept people away. But because it kept people away, my anger was my clutter. I was missing out on the joy of connection with others.

But when I went to college, I started meditating. I would sit by myself, close my eyes, and watch what happened inside me. Sometimes I would sense the presence of things. I experienced a quiet and powerful energy that was everywhere, including in me. As a lovely by-product I became more aware of my emotions.

The new openness I was feeling in college was starting to improve my intuition, which helped saved my ass on a number of occasions. I experienced my intuition after I decided to pledge a fraternity. The frat brothers told me that at some point they would kidnap all the pledge brothers and take us out to the woods in the middle of nowhere and leave us with just a quarter.

One day the fraternity called a special pledge brother meeting, and that morning I decided to put a twenty-dollar bill in my shoe. I went to the house and was immediately jumped on and tied up by the brothers. They took my wallet and cash, but they didn't check my shoes. Rather than tensing up and fighting, I relaxed because I had a feeling that everything would be okay. It felt right to go along with what was happening.

The fraternity brothers loaded five of us pledge brothers into cars. They drove us an hour away to the woods of Maryland. They let us out, untied us, gave us a quarter, and left in a hurry. My fellow pledges were panicked. I told them not to worry. I took off my shoe and showed them the twenty-dollar bill. We walked for fifteen minutes and came to an isolated McDonald's. Outside was a parked cab. The cabbie was inside, smoking a joint and eating a Big Mac. When I asked him if he could give us a ride to Washington, DC, he agreed. He drove us back, going ninety miles an hour, sometimes down one-way streets the wrong way. I was fascinated by how the universe was unfolding this very odd situation.

When we got back to the frat house and went inside, no one was there. We waited, and half an hour later the brothers returned and were stunned to find us sitting there. Openness to my intuition had taken care of all.

When we stop hiding behind the clutter of manufactured might, we become aware of and move with, rather than fighting, the flow of life. I don't mean that esoterically. Clues and answers are naturally built into everyday life. They are kindly placed there to help. When we disregard this assistance, we can't help but screw up. We need all the help we can get. By clutter busting, we gain access to our own built-in support.

Unencumbering Yourself

One of my clients had lived amid the multitudes of musty boxes of stuff in her garage for years. It felt as if she'd been hiding behind all these things, and now that the shell was being removed, she was scared. In fact, living behind things for so long had only made her more fearful and shaky. She was like a person who never exercised because she was scared of being injured, so her body had atrophied and became fragile, almost brittle.

As we sorted through and removed her junk, box by box, I gently encouraged her. I told my client that she looked as though she was coming back to life, that there was light in her face and eyes. I told her that there's strength in being open and delicate. We're so used to thinking that vitality lies in displays of power, but in truth our tenderness and basic sensitivity possess a much greater strength. One clutter-busting workshop participant kept telling me that she felt like she wasn't doing enough. She said, "I want to be supereffective, with a laser focus." The thing is, she was already accomplishing a lot.

I told her that when she said she wanted laser focus, she looked really tired. It was as if her body was holding up a sign that said, "Please stop, I'm exhausted!" It was wearing her out. This way of living was itself clutter because it wasn't giving her the peace of mind she hoped it would.

Hearing this caused her to stop in her tracks. A part of her recognized what she was doing. She took a breath, and the hyperdrive part of her switched off. She relaxed and reconnected to herself. She looked like a whole person.

It's a great thing to learn and grow, but if we do it compulsively, only to make us feel powerful enough to avoid failing or being hurt, we will exhaust ourselves because we will always fail. We can never be powerful enough to avoid that.

The *Today* show recently had their female hosts appear on the air without any makeup. They seemed uncomfortable without their usual layers of face paint and mascara. But they also seemed interesting and real. There was a light coming through their faces that was attractive, and I felt I could connect with them.

When we hide behind the guise of a strong persona, we may feel powerful, but it's a pretension. Deep down, we know it's a show of might that keeps others at bay. It's just not as innately satisfying as simply being ourselves, matter-of-factly and without fear. You are amazing when you are your unencumbered natural self, without trying to hide your faults and hurts. A real person is much more alluring than someone pretending to have it all together.

EXERCISE

Imagine taking off your suit of protective armor as you would your clothes. Notice how much lighter you feel. You're no longer distracted and encumbered by the weight.

- In what way can you give yourself some nurturing attention?
- What can you do now that would make your life more comfortable and peaceful?

Here are some questions to ask yourself:

- Where do I wear armor in my life?
- In what ways do I pretend to be something I'm not?

- What's underneath the layers?
- In what special ways is the light still able to shine from this place within?
- What would it feel like if I uncovered this special part of myself?
- How would I benefit?

The Clutter of Control

The clutter of control occurs when we think someone should change, or we want them to do something for our benefit, even if it's not for theirs — for instance, when we want them to get rid of something we don't like but that they value.

When we try to control another person, we are seeing them as an object. They are no longer a person with feelings but a thing to manipulate. We are familiar with using things as tools to get work done, and sometimes we treat others the same way. If we can cajole, bully, or entice others into doing the things we want them to do, we assume our life will be improved. But these efforts tend to backfire. The impulse behind controlling is often our fear of being hurt by someone, so we subtly and sometimes not so subtly push them for our own protection. This manipulation does not respect or honor the other person, so it undercuts our connection with them.

By nature, people resist manipulation; we all resent attempts to control us. We don't like others judging us and telling us we need to be better people. This is why even if we succeed in manipulating someone else, we tend to feel frustrated, since the other person ends up resenting us, and the distance between us grows.

The same dynamic applies to us. Sometimes we try to force ourselves to be and act a particular way, believing it will help us. This compulsive drive to dominate ourselves can be too harsh. We judge ourselves and hurt our connection with ourselves. We might think this is necessary medicine, but it's clutter because it ends up making us miserable.

I once worked with a client who complained a lot about her weight. When she found pictures of herself, she would say, "I look like a pig," or, "I don't know how I got to be so big! What's wrong with me?" or, "Oh, God, I hate these pictures of myself. I'm so fat." She said she wanted to lose weight and was deeply disappointed that she couldn't. In a disapproving tone, she said she felt that she should be doing better. Her eyes were glazed, and her voice was quiet and sorrowful. She sounded dejected and hopeless. She worried out loud about how she appeared to her friends and family.

I told her that no one notices the things we think are problems. We think people see the things that *we* think are wrong with our lives. But they don't. Chances are they are busy worrying about how others think of them. We are the only ones who see these things as a problem. Sometimes we shame ourselves with relentless criticism as a way to control our behavior.

Some part of her assumed this criticism was necessary as a way to help her lose weight. But it did nothing to help her. Kicking herself in the ass had left her weak and unable to take good care of herself. I said, "I think this critical part of you would be more useful working as a parts inspector on a car assembly line. Then it can find faults all day long and get paid for it."

She laughed. She stopped talking about her weight and started to be more positive. She said, "You know, I think mostly I want to feel more healthy. That would make me happy."

Recognizing our controlling behavior, no matter where it's directed, makes it hard to continue in it. Suddenly, we see that it's not working — and that there's another choice.

The Clutter of Avoidance

When we are uncomfortable, sad, angry, or disappointed, often we want to escape these feelings. We don't think we can handle them. Or maybe we think, "I don't want to be sad. I want to be happy, so I'll get drunk or buy something fun and new." In this way, we try to avoid pain or to distract ourselves from the pain we're already feeling.

Our culture encourages us to buy things to avoid feeling hurt or powerless. We constantly see ads depicting someone who is in some kind of pain. Then that person gets a particular product and becomes happy. The music swells, the actor smiles, the voice-over confidently spouts platitudes.

Things are presented to us as offering instant relief

— a powerful and persuasive message. Most of us are experiencing some kind of pain. We might feel frustrated at work or in a relationship. We might be angry about our financial situation. Our head or stomach aches. When we are in pain, physical or emotional, we are open to suggestions. It's easy to be pulled in by the alluring thought, "If I get _____, then I'll be okay again." We are trained to think and believe this. I know I've thought this many times, especially about new technology.

However, the stuff we get in the hopes of feeling better is clutter unless we really love it. Usually, at best, it provides very temporary relief. Then our unpleasant feelings come back. I remember once feeling really sad and thinking, "I need a pint of Ben & Jerry's Cherry Garcia ice cream." On the container, Ben and Jerry look really happy. There are all those bright psychedelic colors. And then there's the delicious rich, sugary ice cream inside. So I got a pint and ate the whole thing and felt much better. It was like magic. I thought, "This is great!"

The next morning I didn't feel so great, and later in the day I felt worse. I felt sad again, and tired. So I got another pint from my friends Ben and Jerry. This flavor was double chocolate something or other. I ate that and felt good — not great. An hour later I felt sad again, and my stomach hurt. So I stopped buying ice cream.

I also gave up trying to run away. Intuitively, I knew it was impossible to get away from myself, and the awareness brought a powerful sense of relief. I let myself experience and appreciate the sadness, which went from being an unbearable pain to a beautiful sensation. My sadness had a depth and vitality that I hadn't even realized.

Once I saw a commercial that said, "Be even more amazing!" I thought, "Yes!" And then I thought, "Wait. What does that even mean? If I'm already amazing, isn't that enough? And what special qualities and magic powers does this product contain that will increase my amazing quotient?"

While ads have a way of creating a problem where one doesn't exist, in general the desire for something better simply keeps us from feeling satisfied with what we have. Our lives are generally okay. Sure, we might want more of something, but if we got it, pretty soon we'd want more of something else. But what's wrong with accepting our life as it is? With being satisfied with how amazing we are right now? This way of thinking won't stop us from growing, learning, and discovering. The natural urge to change and grow comes from a general sense of happiness, not from a need to acquire things to be happy.

I think we're lucky when we understand that our clutter is not making us happy. Yes, we can enjoy our things. Yes, they do make our lives easier at times. But to believe that things have the power to remove our sadness and make us better people will bring us disappointment and eventually despair.

So, feel sad for a little while. Let anger remain for a moment. Sit with it. Maybe even notice the feelings with some curiosity, like watching leaves falling from a tree. They're a mix of colors, some still partially green, some red, or orange, or yellow, or brown. Then rake the leaves and put them in a bag on the curb. When we don't immediately get some clutter to distract ourselves from what we're feeling, the feelings have a chance to pass naturally.

EXERCISE

One morning you wake up after years of impulsively acquiring stuff. You had a pretty wild time, and now you're feeling tired and dragged out. You notice there are reminders of the blowout strewn about your home. Now it's time to clean up. You get out a trash bag, a donation bag, and a recycling bag and begin to take a look around.

What things did you buy to make you feel high, things that felt exciting to purchase but that you used once or twice, or never, and haven't picked up since? Does something spark that embarrassed, "What was I thinking?" reaction? That's a red flag.

Right now, it doesn't matter that you bought these things. We'll talk about possible reasons later. What helps is knowing that you don't care for them now. It feels really good to pick this stuff up and put it in trash bags. If you don't need it, don't use it, and don't love it, put it in one of the bags. Don't worry about why you bought it; don't worry that you didn't use it or that you don't like it.

You want to feel good *now*. Look through your clothes, your CDs and DVDs, your books. Crack open your cupboards, closets, and drawers. Look for the things that now feel stale and old, that make your head feel foggy. They've lost their vibrancy.

With each thing you find and toss, you will feel that much more sober. It's exciting to feel your feet on the ground again.

The Clutter of Self-Criticism

When I work with people to clear the clutter from their homes and offices, I often hear these very smart people being very mean to themselves. "Why did I screw up like this? I'm such an idiot — why did I do that? I'm so stupid!" It feels so violent. It's as if they are finding the most delicate part of themselves — and punching it as hard as they can. They're punching themselves in the heart. When people do this, their faces become ashen, they lose the brightness in their eyes, and they look sickly. We are all unprotected from this violence because it comes from inside.

It's hard to watch. I sometimes tell my clients, "If

you're going to be mean to yourself, I'll have to charge you triple my usual rate." Keeping things lighthearted helps people open up. If someone else beat them up, they'd resist, but they accept cruelty, harshness, and punishment from themselves. And yet criticism and judgment are never good motivators. When we put ourselves down, we shrink from rather than rising to the occasion. This clutter of self-criticism often invades the process of clutter busting.

When this happens to me, and I get stuck in a task and start to be critical of myself, I stop what I'm doing. I walk away from it because it's painful to use harsh words against myself. So I go for a walk, or I take a nap, or I go to another room and play guitar. You can do similar nourishing things because you love yourself. I know you do, because you care enough about yourself to read this book.

A client once showed me her to-do list, which was many pages long. Her smile was gone. The light in her eyes was out. She hunched over and clutched the papers tightly. It looked like she was trying to protect them in some way. But no one in the room was challenging her. I hadn't even asked her about the lists.

Then she started complaining that she hadn't done anything on the lists. Her voice sounded so tired. She said, "I'm never going to get any of this done! I don't know what's wrong with me. I'm such an idiot. I should be able to do these things. Why do I keep fucking up?" She looked like she was going to cry. She was suffering under the clutter of her criticism.

I told her it was hard for me to watch her kick herself like that. It was as if she was striking herself with lightning bolts. When we put ourselves down, the impact is greater than when someone else does it because the distance is so short.

I said, "Let's take a look at these lists and see if there is anything that really matters to you on them." The first item was reading at night. She felt she needed to read before she went to bed and had a number of books that were "must reading" for her. She hadn't read any of them. When I asked her how long she had wanted to read at night, she told me for at least ten years. I asked her if she likes to read. She said, "Not really." She looked surprised to hear herself say that. When we get a clear look and see that something we thought was gold is instead a turd, we are sobered.

I said, "That's clutter because it's not something you like to do. It's not in your nature. You were hard on yourself because you didn't actually want to do it." She said, "I'd rather spend time with my birds, and meditate, and go to bed early." Two beautiful songbirds chirped in a cage next to her. I said, "You probably don't have to write those things down to do them."

She got up and took out one of her birds from its cage. She sat back down and held the bird. It whistled happily as she rubbed its head and belly. Rather than beating herself up with forced ideas of self-improvement, she took care of herself. This kindness opened her heart to let another being in.

EXERCISE

Get a piece of paper and a pen and sit in a cozy space. At the top of the page, write, "When I get." At the bottom of the page, write, "I'll be happy." Take a deep breath. Look at the space between the two sets of words. You want to write something in the space. But wait. Don't write anything just yet.

Get in touch with your body. Feel your pen hand itching to move. Become aware of increased saliva in your mouth. Feel your heart pumping. Imagine the things you want to write in the space, but wait.

Close your eyes. Feel your breath. Feel the sensations in your body. Be aware of your posture, how you're sitting. Now think about what you have in your life right now that matters to you the most. Feel the powerful connection you have with each thing. Imagine the pain if you lost these things. But wait, they're still there! How lucky are you to have these things in your life?

Open your eyes. Come back to the paper. Look at the space between the phrases at the top and bottom. What do you feel like putting in the space now?

The Noise in Our Heads

We often undervalue ourselves in comparison to others. We praise someone while simultaneously criticizing ourselves. Our underlying motivation is to make ourselves feel miserable enough that we will try harder to improve.

This strategy is clutter because it doesn't inspire us. It weakens us and greatly reduces our capabilities. But it's a hard habit to drop. Comparative demeaning is deeply ingrained in our culture and psyches. It's so instinctual that we are not encouraged to call it into question. But let's take a deeper look.

When we observe others, we see their actions but not their thoughts. We just see a person doing something. This makes them seem focused, strong, clear thinking, and stable. We then compare this to our own efforts at trying to lead our lives amid a loud barrage of critical, sabotaging, fearful, nostalgic, self-doubting, fantasizing, and confusing thoughts. Our thoughts tend to be incessant, illogical, and demeaning. For most of us, if we spoke all our thoughts out loud, we would sound crazy.

But when we observe others, we see their outer life but not their inner — and we assume it's entirely unlike ours. Yet if we were inside their heads, we would hear a voice that sounded strikingly familiar. We would realize that behind someone's quiet, focused demeanor a very different internal monologue is running: one of harsh criticism and petty, envious thoughts. Maybe we would even hear them compare themselves negatively to us. We would seem focused, stable, and clearheaded. In this dynamic, we are more similar to others than we imagine.

Our self-critical comparisons with others are clutter that only emphasizes what's "wrong" with us, not what's right. When we become aware of our outrageous false comparisons, this incessant habit will lessen. "Oh, there goes that thought that I'm worse than everyone else. Is it possible that I could suck that much? It's funny there's such conviction in it. What if that other person is thinking the same crazy thoughts as I am?"

Intuitively you know that everyone wrestles with doubt, confusion, and worry, at least sometimes; these feelings are inescapable. So when observing someone doing something you admire, imagine loud voices of doubt and fear in their heads. Imagine these thoughts at a deafening volume. How does this change your perception of them? Rather than envy, do you start to feel compassion for them as they struggle to be competent? Perhaps you will even feel an affinity with them. By dropping negative comparisons, you can reconnect both with yourself and with others.

The Clutter of Becoming a "Better Me"

I've noticed that a number of recent self-improvement books use the phrase *becoming a better you*. The problem with trying to be a "better you" is the implication that you are not okay now. It also presumes that there's an objective standard of okayness.

Often we want to be "better" so that other people will like us more, or so that we'll like ourselves more. That's clutter. Though we aren't seeking better products, we are seeking better ways of being or better aspects of our personalities. We think, "If I can only become more generous, friendly, smart, creative, wealthy, patient, loyal, honest, funny, lovable, enlightened, or spiritual, then I'll finally be okay." And when we do this, we are reinforcing the feeling not only that we are not okay now, that there is something wrong with us, but also that we need another's approval as proof that we've succeeded. We feel needy, wanting other people's acknowledgment and praise to feel good.

And what do you discover if you succeed in becoming a better you? As it turns out, being liked doesn't change how you feel about yourself. Popular people don't like themselves any more than others like themselves.

I had a client once who told me that she wanted to be a famous author. She felt that, in her career, she had done as much work as others who were well-known. She talked about how different and better her life would be if she had won some literary awards. When she talked about it, she was gone. Her eyes were unfocused, her face was drawn, and she looked tired. She was in a fantasy world.

I described to her how she disappeared when she talked about the need to be liked as a famous person. I said her desire was clutter because it didn't inspire her or open her heart to her work. Plus, it was making her miserable. Whenever we think something in our lives *should* be other than as it is, we drain the present moment of its vitality, which is brutal on our well-being.

My client came to. She said she realized that recognition

would be a burden. She recognized that she'd be exactly the same inside, but she'd have to deal with the headaches of fame. Then she talked about some of the famous people she knew, some of whom were very unhappy. She also realized that her need to be recognized was clutter because it was interfering with her work. Rather than relying on her own intuitive insights when creating, she was thinking about what others would like and approve of.

I became a better me the day I was born.

When a person does something only to be liked — such as forcibly grafting a particular behavior onto themselves while ignoring their own impulses or intuition — they feel disconnected from themselves. Whether or not they win approval, this sense of disconnection often leaves them frustrated, angry, and resentful, which reinforces the feeling that something is wrong with them.

I see this happen a lot. I once worked with a client who was a comedian. She was originally from New York and had a big, vibrant personality. She swore and said whatever was on her mind. When I first came to her apartment, I noticed a metal altar that held a set of Jane Austen's *Pride and Prejudice* VHS tapes. When I asked her about them, she grew pale and quiet. I could see she was wrestling with something inside herself. She said she had constructed this altar as her way of trying to become more feminine. She'd had a string of bad relationships and blamed herself for not being feminine enough. She felt she was chasing guys away with her strong personality. She thought she should be quieter and more delicate, basically a much-reduced version of herself. She was trying to change into what she thought was a more desirable way of being so she could find a better relationship.

I said this particular definition of femininity didn't fit her. It wasn't part of her nature. And if she did somehow figure out a way to forcefully graft that persona onto herself, she would be miserable. I told her she'd be better off being herself and finding a guy who likes her as she is. She laughed hard. She understood what she had been doing and let go of the tapes.

If we're lucky, we get so tired of trying to improve ourselves that we give up. We accept who we are and let go of our fear out of sheer exhaustion. Like Popeye, we declare, "I yam what I yam," and peace of mind follows. The funny thing is, that is a better you. It's the you holding this book, reading this page, feeling weary after years of trying to be amazing, well liked, stronger, all-powerful, and invincible. It's the you who wants to enjoy your life right now as it is. The you who wants to enjoy your relationship with yourself.

Clutter busting is not about creating a better person but about uncovering the wonderful person you are right now. When you take an honest and kind look at all your clutter, you naturally remove the things that don't serve you. You feel better without having to do, be, or have anything else.

What you discover is that your stripped-down, vulnerable, natural self contains an innate happiness.

EXERCISE

Make a list of your good qualities that go unnoticed by others. They can be small or big things that are special to you. They can be the way you observe things or how you think. Maybe it's how creative you are in small ways throughout the day. It can be how you like certain flavors and textures. Perhaps it's your shoes. Or how you find bargains. Maybe it's little insights that you have during the day.

Take a look at the list. This is the list of a special person. What an honor it is for you to know *you*.

The Clutter of Being Right

When we're feeling split off from our connection to ourselves, that estrangement spreads to our other relationships. I see this when I clutter bust couples and they've got two competing opinions about what's right. My sense is that each person has a very strong opinion about what the other should be doing, an opinion that doesn't take into consideration the other person's nature. This dynamic naturally creates distance in the relationship. I talk more about how to deal with this type of clutter in chapter 4, but here I want to take a closer look at how our minds produce the clutter of thinking we are right.

In seeking to understand the world we live in, we develop opinions of all kinds, about cause and effect, about what works and doesn't work, about what we like and don't like. Most important, we distinguish between what feels safe and what feels dangerous. In and of itself, this quality of the mind is valuable. We need to understand the world as best we can to survive, succeed, and protect ourselves daily. But when we fearfully live from the limited perspective of our own isolated alcoves rather than being present in life as it happens, we hurt ourselves. It's very easy to mistake our opinions about life for the truth.

One good way to think about this is to look at the opinions and concepts of our minds as if they were the commentary of a televised sporting event. As the game unfolds, the commentators are in a separate room, high above the event, giving their opinions and feelings about each play. Similarly, life goes about its business while the mind expresses strong opinions and judgments on everything it observes. We think we know the rules of the game, so we interpret everything based on those rules. And most of the time this works. But when we strongly associate with the commentary in our minds, we get a feeling of power over the situation we're observing. This strong connection with our running commentary makes us feel right. When we rely on this way of living, the commentary becomes more important than what's actually happening. In the end, we can't even see the playing field. If we don't recognize this, we will have a hard time understanding what we observe because we won't even be able to see it.

It's a hard habit to drop. I experienced it firsthand when I was a kid. I used to watch football games on TV with my dad. Then one year he began taking me to games. It was weird at first to not hear the incessant commentary. But then it felt relaxing to experience less verbal noise. There was the game, and that was all. Nothing interfered with my experience of what I was seeing, and I felt present with the event. There was the intensity of the play, and there was the quiet space between plays. It was a lovely combination of rest and activity.

At one game there was a guy sitting a row in front of us who had brought a radio with him. He wore earphones so he could listen to the commentary, but I could hear the commentators' voices coming through. This guy seemed more agitated than everyone else. I could sense that he was less present than the people watching the game.

So how do we drop this habit of attaching ourselves to the mind's opinions, judgments, and fantasies? To let go of this clutter, we need awareness. With awareness and an intention to notice, we can begin to experience the contrast between life as it is and our opinions about it. Of course, it's not so simple to turn down the volume of your own mental commentary. It's not easy to start really hearing all the talk that your mind is using to buffer you from the action. But that is how you can start to change, by noticing that it's difficult. Your commentators have been on the air for a long time. But when you start to really hear them, you're not as much under their spell. They don't have the same kind of sway they used to.

Running from a Bony Ghost

When I was a kid, every March my family and I used to go see the Ringling Bros. and Barnum & Bailey Circus. When I was ten, we had seats right by the performers' entrance. I spent a lot of time leaning over the rails and watching whatever was going on backstage. One clown getting ready for his performance fascinated me. He picked up a Styrofoam skeleton that was hanging limply on the wall and calmly attached the skeleton's hands to a brace on his shoulders. The skeleton rested against his back.

Suddenly the lights went down in the hall. A spotlight hit the clown as he ran out of the entrance. The clown ran for his life as the skeleton appeared to be flying after him. You couldn't see the hooks or the harness as the clown looked back in terror at the skeleton, which looked inches away from catching him. The audience was laughing at the poor clown's predicament. The clown ran back into the performers' area. He was calm again as the skeleton lay limply against his back. The clown detached the skeleton and put it back on a rack on the wall. I was fascinated to see the behind-the-scenes mechanics: the truth wasn't always as it appeared.

Flash forward: I was twenty-three and had recently graduated from college. Even though I was still meditating, I was overwhelmed by life. I was used to having my parents take care of me. Now I was completely on my own and uncertain about how to take care of myself. I was worrying a lot. It felt like a helpful activity at the time. I thought that worrying was how one took responsibility. But it made my head so noisy it distracted me from getting helpful solutions from my intuition.

One night I lay on my futon, caught up in the symphony of possible disasters that could befall me, when suddenly everything got quiet. It was as if I'd been listening to really loud music and the electricity had gone off. I was aware of my body vibrating in a weird discordant buzz. My intuition had somehow found a way through all the noise and said, "This is what fear does to my body." The fear I'd been living in had been making my mind and body hyper. I didn't think to find it strange when the fear was happening. I had observed my parents living with fear and thought it was part of life.

Then I remembered the circus. I thought about how, when the clown ran, the skeleton chased him. He could never run fast enough to get away from those ghostly bones. That was me when I was caught up in worry. But backstage, the clown relaxed, hung up the prop skeleton, and walked away calmly. The skeleton was not a real threat. Neither were my fears.

My constantly fearful thoughts had me running for a

salvation that never came. I had been like the clown running from the skeleton. The adrenaline from the fear made
me feel alive. It was like a protective force field. The wor-
ries also made me feel a false sense of safety because I was
alert and ready for the worst to come. But the fearful worrying never brought me relief.

Somehow, I took off my fear and hung it on a peg.
Without it, I was left with life itself in the moment. I felt
peaceful and safe.

EXERCISE

Sit quietly. Listen to your breath. Our breath is
our most important asset. Without it, we can't
experience and enjoy life.

We often ignore our breath because it's simple and basic and always there. It's hard to notice
something when it's constant.

But if something obstructed our breath, we
would do whatever it took to get our breath back.
And when it returned to normal, we would cherish our breath more than anything else.

What are some other simple and integral parts
of your life that go unnoticed, but if you lost them,
you would feel tremendous grief? As you think
of them, take a moment to enjoy their existence.
They are your true wealth.

Let's fondle
everything
we got.

Chapter Two

CLUTTER BUSTING 101

Beneath the chaotic sprawl of our things is space. Not dull, empty space, but space full of lively, vital, and energizing presence. This presence usually goes unnoticed because the chaos of our clutter grabs our attention and distracts us from its nourishing, healing qualities.

What can we do to let go of this clutter and reclaim our space? This chapter gives you an overview of the clutter-busting process. Since this is a 101 chapter, I'll be repeating some of the basics we've already covered, giving them a chance to sink in so they naturally become part of your life. If you want to learn even more, you'll find much more detail in my first book, *Clutter Busting: Letting Go of What's Holding You Back*.

To start, we need to understand what clutter is. To reiterate, clutter is anything in our lives that no longer serves us. It's not just inanimate objects such as piles of paper on our kitchen counters or boxes of old mementos in our garages or closets. Clutter can also be an activity that works against and exhausts us. It can be people we spend time with who make us feel uncomfortable and bad about ourselves, and it can be ways of seeing the world and ourselves that deplete, frustrate, and depress us.

Why don't we just get rid of these things, since they don't work for us? The answer is that we have an emotional attachment to this clutter that makes it difficult for us to let it go. If the reasons that we hold on to something were solely intellectual, then we'd see what was getting in our way and remove it from our lives. But it helps to recognize that our reasons come from a deeper place. It's not necessary to know the subconscious reasons we keep the clutter, but knowing that there is a reason helps us not to blame ourselves for the situation or our resistance and leaves us open to finding a solution.

The solution comes not in examining our subconscious motives but in the simple process of clutter busting. When we clutter bust we ask about each thing in our lives, "Do I use this, or can I let it go?" "Do I love and enjoy this, is it making my life a better place to be, or can I remove it from my life?" "If I were in a store today, would I buy this?" "If I met this person today, would I want to be friends with them?" It's asking whether or not you like something *now*. You are looking for a yes or no answer.

We have an innate ability to know what we like and what we don't. In a restaurant, when we are served a meal, we take one bite and think right away, "Yum" or "Yuck." Usually when people try to solve their clutter situation, they see everything they need to consider all at the same time, it becomes too much, and they give up. Or they buy a storage locker, or a bunch of storage containers, and they hide their things away in an attempt to organize. But these storage units just become expensive trash cans.

From working with hundreds of clients, I have learned that when a person openly considers just one thing at a time, they can think clearly enough to notice whether this thing supports them or whether it's clutter. We work best when we work in this manner. And there are ways to make the process easier on yourself. For starters, I recommend picking one small area to work on at a time:

One file drawer
Just the clothes in your dresser
One cabinet in your kitchen
Only the bookmarks on your computer
The numbers in your cell phone
One stack of papers
Your friends on Facebook
Your car
The hall closet
Your Rolodex
Old emails
One box of stuff

By choosing one area, you are telling your mind to forget about everything else. It then becomes much easier to think and make decisions. You can also set a timer. This helps you say, "For the next hour, I'm just going to focus on this one area. And when I'm done, I'm going to stop."

It's also very useful to move the things you are questioning into a new place. This helps you see them in a new light. We get used to seeing things in their usual places, and even though the clutter may make us uncomfortable, we resist creating a change. You can take that stack of mail, flyers, notes, magazines, and newspapers off the counter and move it to the living room floor. You can take the clothes out of your closet and lay them on the couch, where you will be able to be more flexible and discriminating. But don't just move things around — you also need to go through them!

You can do the clutter-busting process by yourself or with someone else. If you work with another, make sure that they stay impartial and are compassionate. They are there to help by asking you whether or not something serves you and by encouraging you to answer for yourself. It won't work if they tell you what you need to keep or let go of or if they make you feel ashamed or guilty. You want supportive help. I talk more about this in chapter 8.

If you clutter bust by yourself, you will want to support yourself in the same compassionate manner. It doesn't matter how your space got like this. You are here to help yourself. If you spilled a bowl of soup on the floor, you'd clean it up. These things have collected over time, and you are cleaning them up.

While letting go, you may occasionally experience a strong, uncomfortable emotion. This is natural. Living with clutter keeps us constantly distracted. It keeps us from being aware of what's going on in our bodies and minds. When the distractions start to go, we may feel something we've been avoiding. It's best to understand this for what it is: old energy that's moving out of you. It will pass. Stop. Breathe. Be aware of your body as you sit there. Drink some water. As this old energy passes, see if you notice a new strength and openness taking its place.

While you're separating the things that don't support you from what does, make sure not to keep a "maybe" or "not sure" pile. Indecision is a red flag. It means a part of you is saying no to this thing. To get a better grasp of this process, think of something you absolutely love. This item gets a simple yes. You don't have to think about it. That's your guidepost. If you have to defend your need for something, or you go back and forth, or you think, "What if I need it someday?" then this thing is not a part of your life.

When clutter busting, have three trash bags by your side: one bag for trash, another for donation, and the last for recycling. Replace the bags when they get full. And when you are done, remove the clutter from your home. Take the trash out to the cans behind your home, put the recycling in the proper bin, and place the donation items in your car and immediately drop them off at the charity center (or call for a pickup). You can also use www.freecycle.org, where you can list online what you're letting go of and people in the community can write back and ask for it. You want to remove the things that have a toxic effect on your life, and you want to remove them *now*.

As you are clutter busting, stop occasionally and notice the open physical space you're creating. As I've said, space is a tangible thing. Although you may notice all sorts of feelings coming up as you let go, by noticing the calm and supportive qualities of the space, you will be encouraged to keep going.

You are trading the experience of chaos for peace of mind. Once you thought it was better to live with the distracted, jangly energy of too many things. Now you're learning to live with the calming and enlivening presence of just the things you love and all that open space.

It's very important, when you are finished working in one area, that you resist the temptation to fill up the empty space. Don't put anything in it right away. Take the time to make friends with the space. It may feel odd at first, but you will get used to the openness.

The Benefits of Space

We need open and unencumbered space inside and outside us just as much as we need food and sleep. Sometimes we don't realize this until we begin to let go of clutter and notice how good we are starting to feel.

I was once helping a client clutter bust her storage locker of remnants from her old business. There were stacks of old flyers, business cards, and prospect sheets; old musty business books; and motivational cassettes. Her mind was flooded with memories of the past and things that might have been. She felt hopeless. But as I gently asked her how she felt about each thing, she began to let go and get some clarity. As the space opened up, her self-confidence returned, and she found that she was able to let go of all the old business artifacts. She sensed that she was letting go of the assumption that she needed her old stuff to prove that her life had substance. The true substance was the open and alive space inside her that was emerging. Open space, like oxygen, was coming in and reinvigorating her.

As people find and let go of what doesn't fit in their homes and in themselves, as they create more open space in their lives, they feel happy again — not happy simply because they have more space but because the space supports, comforts, relaxes, and revitalizes them.

You can find and determine the right amount of open space for you. A room doesn't need to be stripped of everything for us to be aware of and receive the benefits of space. Not all our things are clutter. Clutter busting isn't simply about throwing things away; it's about refining our discernment. As you find and let go of things that no longer serve you, you can feel the ease coming back into your body and mind. As the chaos goes, you notice the peace of mind within the space of *you*. What remain are only those things that are an essential part of your life in an open space that nourishes you.

I once worked with a couple who were feeling distraught in their chaotic bedroom. Their nightstands were spilling over with papers and books. The space under their bed was jammed with more papers, storage containers, photos, and clothes. The husband's work desk, clogged with papers, was inches from their bed. The couple complained about not being able to sleep well. I told them that the bedroom needs to be a peaceful sanctuary where they can retreat from the world and recharge.

The couple took this to heart and let go of anything that wasn't soothing and supportive. They moved the desk out, cleaned everything out from underneath the bed, and left only a lamp and a book they loved on their nightstands. They couldn't believe how much more peaceful the room felt to them. They were so startled that they had to call their friends and say, "You're not going to believe how great our bedroom feels. You need to come over now!" Their friends drove over right away. They came upstairs, looked around, and said, "Oh, my God! I can't believe how wonderful it feels in here!" It was the first time I'd ever experienced people getting excited about peacefulness!

EXERCISE

We don't normally notice space — we notice the things in our space and get lost in the distractions of the clutter. I think of space as a supportive container for the things you love.

Imagine that you have an inner detector that senses the presence of space. Turn on your space detector and walk into a room. See if you notice the space supporting everything. The space is quieter than the things it holds, but you are aware of its presence. You may even sense your connection with this presence. Notice that this space is within you too.

Now look around the room: Does something keep you from tapping into the space when you come into the room? Does something make you feel tired or edgy? Does something fit awkwardly or seem unnecessary? Sometimes it helps to look out of the corner of your eye. This allows your thinking mind to become less dominant and your intuitive knowingness to rise to the occasion.

Pick up anything that stands out, and remove it from the room. Come back in and feel the space again. Is your connection to the underlying space changed in any way? Is it stronger or more positive?

Keep going in this way, sensing and removing anything else in the room that distracts you until you have reconnected with the enlivening space underneath.

A Short Explanation of "Why"

In the preceding chapter, we talked about some of the reasons why we hang on to things, and it's good to remember them as we clutter bust. Often we buy or bring things into our lives because of the promise that these things will make our lives more exciting and valuable. True enough, acquiring things inspires a brief period of excitement. But this excitement quickly fades, and we end up feeling dulled, neurotic, and needy. We experience a "stuff hangover."

Despite the presence of all these things we thought were going to "do it" for us, we still feel something is missing. Rather than noticing that things aren't the solution, we continue to look for something else to make us feel better.

The same goes with our personalities: we acquire attributes and ways of being because they promise to make us more enticing and powerful. But it's impossible to maintain something that's not in our true nature. We exhaust ourselves in an attempt to "be better," filling up our interior lives with clutter, and we end up feeling frustrated and inadequate.

The Emotional Benefits of Letting Go

One of my clients sat gloomily in her home office amid piles of papers. At her feet were bills, letters that needed her response, articles she had torn out of magazines to read, notes she had scrawled to herself, event flyers, papers that needed filing, and photographs. She was overwhelmed and started to cry. Then she said, "I'm so embarrassed that I'm crying."

I told her that crying was no extra charge, and she laughed. I said that she looked alive when she cried. When I had first arrived she looked comatose, but when she started to feel, she came alive.

After weeping for a while, she began to go through

her papers, sniffling as she worked. I could see that she was operating more clearly. She was aware of the things in front of her. She threw out papers she didn't need. She paid bills online. She mailed things that needed mailing. She made a few calls that needed to be taken care of. She started to smile.

When people open up and stop trying to cover up who they are, their vulnerability is powerful. They've come back to life.

You may find yourself feeling powerful emotions while you clutter bust. That means your body and mind are naturally letting go of old, trapped emotions. The discomfort you feel is the sensation of their leaving you. Imagine that the old emotions are just passing through. And since they don't feel good, it's nice to know they won't be sitting inside you anymore. You don't need to analyze them. You can be curious and notice them. Maybe you'll even get some insights. The greater benefit is that once they've left, you'll feel lighter and see things more clearly.

Experiences Are Our Gold

As we begin to shed the clutter armor that keeps us from connecting with ourselves, we relax and begin to notice and appreciate life anew.

Once that armor starts to fall away, life becomes the universe's big assembly line of new experiences coming directly into our lives. Every day new things and intuitive insights float right in, transforming us. We begin noticing the subtler moments and events that are happening all the time: the way sunlight strikes the table, how we feel moment to moment, how the people around us are changing and growing, what it sounds like when we breathe.

Life itself becomes fascinating because we're establishing a relationship with everything around us. We no longer live like a separate person fighting for what we want against an uncompromising universe. We're part of the whole, but not in an intellectual or New Agey sense. We're not forcing the concept of being connected to everything, but we find the experience happening to us anyway. This openness and connection happen naturally when we clutter bust. It's a tangible and natural feeling of belonging.

Without the incessant distraction of our clutter, we find ourselves treasuring the experiences that feed us right now, rather than relying on our memories of the past or our hopes for the future. We become less interested in acquiring things because, no matter how valuable those things may be, we get greater satisfaction from the experience of love in our lives.

We now see that we were trained to think that our things are more important than our experiences. As we learn to value our experiences, the excitement over acquiring, possessing, and holding on to *tangible things* starts to fade. I remember one client, during the middle of a clutter bust, saying to me, "This is going to save me a lot of money because I'm done buying all this crap!"

When we notice our experiences, we connect to our environment. This makes us happy. You won't see this connection advertised. It's rarely talked about, and it can't be bought or sold. It doesn't need a marketing department. There's charm inherent in our experiences because they are us. Our experiences, like us, are sacred; they are our gold. And nothing else comes close.

Recognizing Your Connection with Your Things

We have a relationship with everything in our life. When we clutter bust we recognize and consider each relationship: Is it helping me right now, or is it hurting me?

When something is part of our life, it's no longer just a thing. It becomes an experience we have a connection with. If it's a shirt we love, we enjoy wearing the shirt. The shirt feels good on our body. We feel good when we see our-selves in the mirror. We feel joy when we take the shirt off the hanger and put it on. We have a tangible relationship with the shirt. And if we were clutter busting our closet, we would keep this shirt.

Similarly, you would keep anything you own that you appreciate and enjoy and use. You enjoy driving your car. You appreciate your cell phone. Your computer makes life easier. You love your interactions with your friends. You relish the fresh food you take out of your exceptional fridge and cook on your amazing stove and eat with your favorite silverware and plates. You're not pretending to like these things — you do like them. It gives you joy to interact with the things that matter to you. It's good to remember to appreciate all the useful things that aid us in our lives.

It's the same with people: If we love the interactions with our friends and family, then there's no problem. These are relationships to keep and appreciate.

Things that we don't use, that we don't care for, and that make us feel bad about ourselves are clutter. Maybe these things once enthralled us, or we really wanted to enjoy them, or someone said we would love them, or an ad said they would make us a better person...but in reality we are not *enjoying* them right now. These objects don't help us in any tangible way. Our relationship with these things creates stagnation in our lives. We don't need to go into couples' therapy with our clutter. We need to let it go.

I once worked with a clutter-busting client who had a

very vibrant personality. But when we came across three boxes of college memorabilia that had been hiding out in her attic and that she hadn't looked at in seventeen years, her vitality disappeared. It was as if she had gone from being a shining sun to being gloomy and overcast. She said college was the last time she had felt special, and yet experiencing it again right now was making her feel like her current life was worthless. My client's drastic response was a red flag indicating the stagnant effect of her bad relationship with her college stuff. I pointed out the giant shift in her way of being, and she sobered up and got it. She decided she didn't want the adverse side effects of the college clutter, and she let the stuff in the boxes go. Naturally, letting go in the context of a relationship with a person is trickier, but it is similar, as we will explore in more detail throughout this book.

For now, when clutter busting your own stuff, notice the relationship you have with your things, particularly the things that matter to you. Do they give you life and inspire joy in you? Sometimes it's obvious. Many times we have overlooked simple things and forgotten to appreciate them.

Now notice the contrast with the objects in your life that don't bring joy. These are the things in your environment that you don't interact with, that you no longer care for, and/or that actually hurt you. We're pretty simple creatures. Something either brings us pleasure or dulls us. It's okay to extract the stagnant things from our lives. It's very much like trimming dead leaves from a houseplant. When we do, the healthy parts of the plant benefit.

EXERCISE

Does anything come to mind as you read about things feeling stagnant in your life? Do you see any images or get an intuitive nudge?

If so, a quiet part of you is telling you something. Go to the thing. Remove it from its place and hold it in your hands. Does this thing still feel alive to you? Is there a vibrant connection, or is it a dead branch that needs to be pruned to help the living tree thrive?

Working through Resistance with Kindness

Giving yourself permission to let go of what doesn't serve you is very powerful. You will become highly energized. People who have done clutter busting on their own have told me about how they embraced the process and were freely tossing things that were no longer a part of their lives. They were enjoying the feeling of openness and freedom. Then suddenly they felt an emotional storm rise up. They lost their connection, it became too much, and they stopped the clutter bust.

Clutter busting is an intimate process. Our sensitivity is on high. Suddenly we come across something that has powerful emotional associations for us. We are used to seeing things through the haze of distractions. Our diversions create an emotional distance that makes us feel safe. But now we are receiving the full impact, and it's overwhelming. We shut down to protect ourselves.

People often judge themselves for closing up. I tell them it's a natural reaction. We are sensitive creatures. If we sense we could get hurt, we automatically protect ourselves. When you see resistance in yourself, react with compassion. Be kind and take a break. Getting a glass of water, sitting quietly, or stepping outside for a second takes our attention away from the tough emotions we are feeling and allows them to run their course.

While we clutter bust, we may feel afraid: "I'm scared of the space being created — I'm scared to clear away the distractions because I fear that what remains won't be my intuitive, loving self, but this mad self that has a headache from being buried under so much clutter."

Here's what's critical to know when you meet resistance: the fear comes *from* being buried alive under clutter. Living under the oppression of clutter distorts our hearts. It helps to kindly remind yourself that you're taking the time to let go of one thing at a time and that you're staying in touch with yourself during the process. You won't abandon yourself during this process. Speaking with yourself gently helps the fear fade away.

Doing the opposite, being hard on ourselves and treating ourselves harshly, only makes us feel more overwhelmed. Criticism doesn't help us function well; we make mistakes. I see my clutter-busting clients often getting upset at themselves for not finishing things. But under that feeling of upset, I sense their frustration. The upset is a way of covering up the vulnerability of frustration. It's hard to admit to being vulnerable. It means accepting that we are sensitive and tender, which can be scary. It means we could get hurt. But the thing is, we're already hurt. And keeping the clutter around will hurt us even more.

So I'm easy on my clients. I don't demand anything from them. I keep it simple and encourage them to be kind to themselves. We all need encouragement. Analyzing why we are wrong keeps us connected to the disorder. Encouragement brings back kindness and puts the clutter bust back on track.

When you're feeling overwhelmed and you notice that you're compulsively pushing yourself, you can ask, "Do I need a break? Would a nap help? Perhaps I should eat something?" Or, "Could this be simplified?" It's all right to think, "I'm tired. I need a treat. I really need some encouragement. Nothing is important enough to make me feel this bad. I need a break."

One of my clients was a supervisor at a large company. She was feeling stressed and fearful that she wasn't doing enough. She was angry with herself for not being able to keep up with the workload. She said that she got so busy at her job that she wouldn't even give herself bathroom breaks.

I said, "Do you have to go now?" She had to think about it. She said, "Yes!" I said, "Okay, let's go." She said,

"I can go later. Look how long my to-do list is!" I said, "Yes, *this* is the first thing on that list." I said that when she doesn't take care of herself, her work suffers. When that happens, she's harder on herself. It's a vicious circle with no end in sight. She paused, then got up and went to the restroom. When she came back, she sat down at her desk in a new frame of mind. She actually came up with some solutions to some of her problems at work.

Being kind to ourselves is a skill. It's as important as anything we could learn in business school. We can be pretty hard on ourselves. We think being that way motivates us. Or we were taught that change comes through force. But criticism is ineffective. It creates resistance and tension and makes us cower within.

We don't need any more reasons to chastise ourselves. Blame erases our connection with ourselves, while kindness, treating ourselves with compassion, is an elixir restoring our basic connection with ourselves and others.

I find it's best to treat clutter busting as an invitation. We must be open to the process, or at least curious, for it to work. We can't force ourselves to clutter bust. Resistance prevents us from experiencing the nonjudgmental awareness that's necessary in recognizing whether something should stay or go. As we'll see a bit later, approaching clutter busting as an invitation is doubly important in relationships.

Often when people find out that I do clutter busting, they say, "I can't have you over. You'll be telling me I need to get rid of everything." The funny thing is, when I pay a social visit to someone's home, I never see clutter, nor do I feel a need to suggest tossing. When someone does hire me, my clutter-busting radar kicks in, and I jump into it because their openness compels me. They have *invited* me in.

None of us can be forced to be open. Pushing, demanding, threatening, and scaring never make people change in a positive way. They may do something differently because they are intimidated or afraid. But it won't benefit them or us. When we use those same tactics on ourselves, the results are equally perilous.

In contrast, the openness that allows change to happen comes from a spontaneous, natural reaction inside us. Suddenly we feel we want to do something different. "I can't keep doing things this way. It's too painful. I want to do something about this." It takes that kind of realization to fuel us to do something positive.

I once got an email from someone who wrote, "I spent most of my life living in the hell of my clutter. I hated it. I felt guilty about it. I told myself I have to do something about it. But nothing changed. And then there were the people telling me I had to do something about it. My family would give me books on organization every Christmas. They refused to come over unless I did something about it. But nothing happened. And then one day I got this feeling that I had a chance to be happy without all this stuff. I just knew it. It was a simple feeling. It wasn't me beating myself over the head. It was a permission to start. So I began to let go of what I wasn't using, and I began to feel better."

I invite you to let the process in and begin clutter busting your life.

I went crazy
until I found
it didn't take
me any where.

Chapter Three

CLUTTER AS A DEFENSE

My client's basement was filled with stacks of clothes and boxes of papers. Her husband came by as we began to work. He clearly didn't approve of what she was doing.

He said to me, "You're just wasting your time. She's not going to be able to get rid of anything." She shrank at his words and disconnected from him. I think he sensed this, and it hurt him, but to protect himself he grew even harsher with her. He said, "You can't do without all of your stupid crap. If you do throw something out, you're just going to go out and buy more crap. You're throwing away money." She was on the verge of crying, so I asked him to leave.

After he left, she burst into tears. She didn't want to do the clutter busting anymore. I said her husband had treated her badly just then because he's scared of her strength. Whenever someone attacks another person for trying to improve their life, they are scared that they will no longer be able to control that person. She reacted to his bullying and shut down. I told her I wanted to work with the strong part of her. She accepted, and we went back to work.

We worked diligently. I encouraged her to be relentless in her tossing, and she was. Her clarity helped her see whether or not something served her. She recognized that she no longer wore most of her clothes, and she bagged them up for charity. She had no need of most of the papers in her basement, and they went into bags for recycling. When we were done, she admired all the new space she'd created. She said, "I think I kept all this stuff down here because on some level I knew it really bothered him. It was kind of like me saying a big 'fuck you' to him. But I don't feel angry anymore."

When we were done, her husband came back downstairs. He saw a mostly empty basement. He didn't say anything. His mouth actually hung open. He was expecting to humiliate her and was stunned. Instead of disparaging her efforts, he put his arm around her and said, "I'm so proud of you. You did an amazing job." She burst into happy tears. He kept looking around and saying, "This is just incredible."

Sometimes a spouse is threatened by their partner's letting-go process. The couple may be emotionally stuck, and for whatever reason, a spouse may not want the other to change their behavior. Perhaps they simply fear change, or perhaps they are invested in the way things are, and so they prefer to control and dominate the other. Sometimes, spouses will try to derail the work, and this is why I initially asked the husband to leave. My client couldn't work when she felt threatened by him.

However, when we were done, my client acknowledged something interesting: she had used her clutter as a way to express her anger toward her husband. Her mess was a nonverbal message. Though their argument probably didn't start with the clutter, her unspoken message helps explain the husband's defensiveness: he understood on some level that the clutter represented his wife's anger at him. Even the wife didn't fully see this until she was done, only after she'd let go of the clutter and her anger at the same time. Then, her husband's reaction was proof of her success: he felt safe enough to open his heart and embrace her.

Sometimes, our clutter isn't only about us. This may be the reason it's so hard to clean up certain messes, for we use the clutter to send a message. This message is our secret justification for the clutter, the reason we defend and protect certain objects. When clutter is really communication, whether conscious or not, whether aimed at others or ourselves, letting it go means letting go of the reason we think we need it. It means learning to speak clearly with ourselves and others.

Giving by Letting Go

I was working with a couple who had been cold and cautious with each other. There was a feeling of animosity underlying their words, with no ease of love between them.

We were working in their living room, when suddenly

she said, "There's something I want to say." Her emotions rose to the surface and she tried fighting back tears. But they flowed. A tremendous amount of anger and sadness poured from her.

She said, "We used to have a problem with alcohol. It was destroying our lives. So we decided to stop drinking. We haven't had a drink since. But my husband has a case of wine that he keeps in the base of a cabinet my dad made for our wedding. He said he's saving it for when he feels it's okay for him to start drinking again. I don't like having it in the house. I've told him this, and he won't listen to me." She couldn't look at her husband when she said this. I sensed she feared his reaction.

He was startled. He said, "You told me it was okay to keep it." She said, "I did, but I don't feel that way anymore. I want it out of here!" He said, "But you said I could keep it!"

She continued to cry while he remained silent.

The husband and wife had opposing feelings about the wine, and both wanted to control the other. Meanwhile, each resisted the other's attempts. They were stuck, and their openness was gone. It sounded as if it had been this way for a while. As usual, my approach was to help each of them hear what the other was saying and get them to drop their defenses. When couples get back to their own connection with themselves, the best solution for dealing with clutter typically reveals itself.

To help get them there, I decided to repeat what each partner had said they wanted. I said to the woman that she didn't want her husband to have alcohol in their home. It had destroyed their life some years ago, and she didn't want to put her family at risk again. She was asking her husband to help her protect their family.

I said to the husband that he felt angry that she had told him one thing and then changed her mind and told him another. To him, the wine was like a promise that one day he would be better; it represented his hope that one day he could handle having a drink again. I said they were both angry at each other and didn't feel listened to.

He said, "I don't understand. She said I could keep it. I'm not even going to drink it unless I feel it's okay." She yelled at him, "Our drinking almost destroyed us. I want it out of the house!"

I reminded her that she was in pain because of the alcohol in their home and the threat it embodied. I reminded him that he loved his wife, and yet he wanted her to trust him about this.

He said, "But I'm not going to drink."

I felt that the wife had stopped trying to control him and had become very direct and present about her basic feelings. The husband hadn't. I thought that if I could help him be direct with himself, it would help him to snap out of it.

The wife was in genuine pain. If she had just stepped on a piece of glass, her husband would have run to get antiseptic and a bandage and taken care of her. If necessary, he would have taken her to the hospital without hesitation because it feels good to take away the pain of someone we love.

Meanwhile, the husband's reason for keeping the wine was all about the future. He wanted to keep open his option to drink it someday. But keeping it entailed a risk for everyone. What if he started drinking again and the same problems returned? That would put his family in danger. What if his wife was tempted by its presence and took a drink, when she was committed to *never* drinking again?

I told the husband that he put his wife and daughter at great risk by keeping the wine in the house. Whatever purpose the wine served for him, the presence of the wine in their home was not serving his family, so ultimately it couldn't serve him.

He finally looked at her. He could see the pain in his wife's face. His heart opened, and there was finally a connection between them.

He said to her, "This is hurting you?" She said, "Yes." He said, "Okay, I'll let it go." She said, "Thank you." There was a beautiful, deep tenderness between them. No matter how right and justified we may feel about an object, it never feels bad to let it go if we do so with compassion for those we love.

EXERCISE

No one wants to be controlled. When someone tries to control us, it feels as if they see us as a car they can drive. We sometimes counter that by trying to steer the other person in a different direction. It's a mess!

If this is happening with someone you live with, particularly if you are arguing over things, this exercise will help you learn to be open with the other person and not manipulate them. It takes concerted focus to learn how to be gentle together.

First, tell the person about your discomfort. Talk about it as if you were physically uncomfortable. Describe your experience. Tell them you would like to feel better about your communication and your connection with them. Ask if they would like to participate in a clutter bust as a way to learn how to work together.

If they agree, find a neutral person you are

both comfortable with, and ask them to come over and ask you both about the things in your home — without judgment. By having an impartial person assisting you, you both get the chance to say how you feel about each item that you go through. You get to communicate and be heard.

We're often on better behavior when someone else is around. This is a chance to try out the better behavior with the person you are close with. You might find that it makes you feel better

When you ask the person to help you out in this way, offer to repay them with a nice dinner. You want to show them that you appreciate their efforts. When they come over, tell them that their job is to pick one area, and then select one item at a time and ask each of you, "Do you like this, or can you let it go?" This person is like an encouraging survey taker. They should repeat back what each of you says so you both feel that you have been heard.

Clutter busting is a way to slow down how we interact and feel, so we can sidestep the reactionary part of ourselves and get a chance to see and experience how we actually feel. By clutter busting with the person you share space with, you also get to see the mechanics of how you interact with this other person. Your relationship with them is as much a thing as each item you are going through. By being aware of ways you interact that are caustic, you get a chance to heal your relationship.

If the person you live with doesn't want to do the clutter bust, don't push it. Just the fact that you expressed your feelings in a nonthreatening way is a positive gesture. You're learning how to take care of yourself and to be kind to the people you are close with.

Shackle-Free

Sometimes those we don't share space with can control us, even at a distance. They have a powerful influence on our behavior. Even when these controlling people are no longer in our lives, we may continue the behaviors we learned from them. Our clutter can be a response to one of these controllers. When this happens, we need to recognize that we are the only ones keeping ourselves from realizing our intuitive, connected self in the present moment.

My client was embarrassed to show me her home office, which was in a small laundry room. The house was huge, but she had relegated herself to this tiny space. The washer and dryer were on the left side. On the right, under a mound of paper, was her small desk. Boxes stuffed with miscellaneous papers were piled on the floor. All the shelves were crammed with papers, office supplies, books, and various other things. It felt like a prison cell. I got a clue about what was going on when she called it the "control center." She also called it her nightmare.

She blurted out, "Oh, my God, I never get anything done!"

My client was critical of herself for letting things get to such a cluttered state. Her personal assessment was harsh, even cruel, and I pointed this out to her. She said she grew up hearing the same criticisms from her mother. She ended up letting her mother make most of her decisions for her. When she grew up and left home, she got married and her husband took over the job of criticizing and controlling her. Her husband was traveling at the moment, so the only person being critical at that moment was she.

I told her I thought she was very powerful but that she had gotten used to diminishing herself to make others happy. This sometimes happens to powerful people. Those around them are scared of their strength and try to dominate them. The powerful person reduces themselves to preserve the relationship. My client learned at a young age to be small to make her mom okay with her. That's probably why she held herself back with the clutter in that room. It sapped her strength and kept her tiny.

We don't look good with shackles on. They don't suit us, and they don't really help anyone. It doesn't matter how long we've held ourselves back or who we held ourselves back for. We know we can't live that way anymore. It feels better to be free. We like to shine, and shine big.

With strength returning to her voice, my client told me, "I'm so tired of shrinking to fit in. I think I did it to avoid my mom's anger and pain. She's been ruling over me as a ghost through my husband. There's no peace in living that way for me. I'm not some kind of idiot that needs to be taken care of. I know what's right for me. I really want to start enjoying my life. I have a lot of things I want to do." It was exciting to see her coming back to life.

This woman's clutter was her way of "obeying" her mom, of diminishing herself and keeping the peace. But she did this at the expense of her own inner peace. For her, letting go of clutter meant becoming life-size again.

From this place of strength, my client quickly let go of a majority of the papers. Because she was thinking clearly, she saw they were superfluous. She also decided to move the desk, office supplies, and books to a spare room upstairs, where she would have more space and comfort. Without the limitations of her emotional clutter, she was powerfully taking care of herself.

Once we get our innate self-confidence back, we can take really good care of ourselves and, from this place, create our life. We reestablish our relationship with ourselves, which forms the basis of healthy and joyful partnerships with others.

Protection That Hurts

I was working with a client in her condo. Her stuff covered her floor, and there was no place to walk. We had to step on and over things to get around. My client went to work every day. But then she came home and rarely left the house again. She wanted to get out more, but she just couldn't do it.

I noticed that she didn't interact with most of the things in her home. Many packages were still in their original wrappers. She didn't feel at home in her own house. She seemed unsettled. She'd sit on the edge of her couch, and her eyes would dart around a lot. She looked like a hunted animal.

I told her that all the things in her home were the ingredients of her fortress. A fort is meant to keep out invaders. The thing is, no one was trying to attack or hurt her. There were no invaders. I said, "It turns out you were already safe. But now the fort has become a problem." It was hard for her to hear this because she'd become invested in living this way. I told her it was natural to defend her fort because she'd spent a lot of time building it. But the fact that she had hired me meant that she knew her home was her real enemy.

My client told me that she was estranged from her mother. Throughout her life, her mother had been very controlling, judging her negatively over the decisions she made. My client ended up shutting her mother out of her life. But this also was hard for her. She missed her mother, and she felt sad and frustrated about the whole situation.

I had her make a fist. I told her to keep making the fist. After thirty seconds she said her hand was starting to get tired. I said, "That fist is protecting the inside of your hand. Nothing outside you is trying to hurt the soft and sensitive part of your hand. But notice that the fist is actually what's hurting your hand." At my words she shook out her hand.

My client had shut down and isolated herself as a way to protect herself from her mother. But this living fist was hurting her. It cut her off from her heart and her connection with her mom. I suggested that if she lived with openness again, she might come up with a new and better way to have a relationship with her mother. I asked her if she was open to trying to live a different way. She said yes.

I got out a trash bag and started asking her about the things on the floor. I showed her only one thing at a time, asking gently whether or not she liked it. I kept it simple, so she could feel her connection to her things while remaining emotionally connected to herself.

My client ended up dismantling her fort. The new, open space made her feel much more present. I think the openness made her feel safer. When we're fearful, openness is scary. But when we see that we're not in danger, being open allows our natural power to emerge. We learn to trust that we can protect ourselves when we need to.

She said she felt strong enough to approach her mother with an open heart and decided to send her some flowers. For her, this was a new message, an uncluttered one, and one that didn't hurt.

Anatomy of a Buffer

My client was intimidated by her husband. She and her kids were afraid of his angry outbursts. They tiptoed around him because little things would set him off. She told me the story of the time she took a pair of beat-up old running shoes that he wasn't wearing and gave them to a homeless person. When he found out he threatened to divorce her.

As a result, she was afraid to go near his things. As we clutter busted, she steered clear of her husband's vast collections of books, records, CDs, DVDs, and other things, and yet these took up a lot of space in the house.

His anger acted as a growling personal guard dog that kept everyone away. It also kept away the experience of love and connection. It intimidated his wife so much that she spoke about it in a whisper so that he wouldn't hear, even though he wasn't even at home while we worked.

I suspected that deep down her husband was a sensitive person who was afraid of being hurt. His anger was a defense. People who get easily overwhelmed by their feelings often create a protective buffer around themselves. They use this kind of clutter in relationships to keep others at a distance. I've found that, typically, the anger can make them feel big and powerful when they are actually scared. They're very fragile. The louder the bark, and the higher the walls, the greater the fear.

When we are scared by our sensitivity, we bring distractions — clutter — into our lives. Since we can't choose not to have emotions, we feel we need to surround ourselves with protective things that keep us from feeling them. This way, our attention goes to the things rather than to our feelings. It's an attempt to control the overwhelming sensations.

I told my client that when she threw out her husband's

old, beat-up running shoes, he became irrational because she took away one of his buffers. He felt naked and vulnerable, and this probably made him panic. The shoes were one of the many things he surrounded himself with that acted as an anesthetic. When they were gone, suddenly he was flooded with feeling. This was too much for him, and he reacted strongly as a protective gesture.

I said this matter-of-factly. I wasn't trying to justify his behavior, only to explain it in the context of my clutter-busting experience. She was living in a constant state of fear because of his anger. Often in relationships we react to someone else's intensity with equal intensity. This emotional reaction is *our* protective buffer. It's like two buffers are talking to each other, not two people. And yet, despite all these defenses, no one feels truly safe.

Dropping our defenses doesn't mean willfully putting ourselves in danger — we don't stand in the middle of the road and let a car run us down. But there are kind ways we can take care of ourselves in our relationships. The way to begin is with an open recognition of what's happening. "This person lashed out at me. I can feel myself hiding from them and wanting to stay hidden." Awareness creates a sense of calm. Perspective returns.

During clutter-busting sessions, I've seen this awareness lead to amazing turnarounds. If someone overreacts emotionally to a perceived threat of losing an object, and I react calmly, with openness and understanding, then they have a chance to see their reaction for what it is: protective fear. They see that this fear is keeping them from connecting with themselves and others. This awareness opens the situation for new opportunities to come in. Then change can happen.

When my client saw what was actually happening between her and her husband, she seemed to relax. I noticed she was taking in more breath and no longer hunched her shoulders. Her eyes went from a squint to being open and bright. She was beginning to drop her buffer. The contrast appeared to startle her.

She said, "I see that he pretends to be strong with his anger. That must be really hard for him to maintain. I think he must be really exhausted inside. Wow, it's weird, but I don't feel scared of him anymore."

Clutter as a Distraction

I was working with a client who was also experiencing marital problems. We were in his home office, where there were many piles of papers, magazines, and various things on the floor. They also covered his desk and couch. He couldn't relax in the space. He worried that he had made such a mess of things that he couldn't fix them. He was feeling scattered and couldn't sit still.

My client had some guitars hanging on the walls. I took one down and made up a song about the clutter, which helped him relax a little. Then I got out a trash bag and started asking him questions about the items on the floor. As it usually goes, many things turned out not to be important to him. His anguish began to dissipate as we went through the piles.

In the midst of the tossing, he began to get stuck again. His emotions took over. So I started asking him questions about his life. He told me that he was having problems in his relationship with his wife. I said that perhaps he attracted this clutter to distract him from the difficult situation that was hurting his heart.

Physical clutter is distracting. It involves a lot of our attention, and sometimes we create it deliberately — we create a false problem to cover up our bigger problems. But this ruse doesn't work very well, and we usually end up with two problems: the original problem and the clutter that was supposed to distract us from it.

I told my client that by removing the clutter he was uncovering the difficult emotions concerning his marriage that he'd been avoiding. If the reason for the clutter was to create a distraction, then removing the distraction left him facing his original troubles. When we try to cover up our pain with more pain, we often confuse the source. It's as if you hit your head on a beam, and to take your mind off your headache, you deliberately stub your toe. Now both your toe and your head hurt. No wonder you feel bad.

Then maybe you think, "If I just heal my toe, I'll be okay." But this self-inflicted problem isn't your real predicament. We focus all our energy on the false problem, thinking it's the cause of the pain, but it's not. As the toe heals, the awareness of our original injury returns, and so we stub our toe over and over, avoiding the real issue by creating the same false one. We seem to have lost track of our underlying problem, but we still feel the pain from it.

When I explained these ideas to my client, he started to laugh. When we see the big picture of the unconscious bizarre things we do to avoid pain in our relationships, it can seem humorous. It's fascinatingly convoluted.

He said, "I get why I had all this clutter around me. It made me less present around my wife. I'm sure that didn't help things. I think it just made her madder at me, and that probably just made me add more crap to the piles. I don't care about any of these papers around me. I miss my wife."

What message had his clutter been sending to his wife? In essence, "I don't want to deal with you." Of course, no one likes to hear that, and her anger only hurt him more, and this drove him further into the distraction of his clutter.

And what was the underlying hurt he was trying to distract himself from? He was afraid his wife didn't love him. He was scared, and he had tried to cut off the fear by piling up clutter. But when we cut off uncomfortable feelings, we cut off the enjoyable ones too. Either we are connected to our emotions or we are not, and if we lose our connection with ourselves, that disconnection spreads to our other relationships too.

Through clutter busting, my client was able to stop and see what he was doing. Not in a blame-filled, "Why the hell am I doing this?" way, but with nonjudgmental awareness, even curiosity. Once he recognized the clutter for what it was, and the true harm it was causing him, he could let it go.

This process is all about having an open curiosity about what's happening. If we're harsh with ourselves in our introspection, we'll react by shutting down, basically creating another distraction. That may happen anyway, but if we're observing ourselves, we'll notice that a distraction is occurring. The noticing and curiosity will create openness again, allowing us to see. These are the steps toward a kinder, more effective approach to change.

A Cluttered Habit

My client was experiencing difficulty in his relationship with his girlfriend. He was also thinking of having an affair with a woman he'd been flirting with online. When he was talking about his situation, he looked away from me, and his eyes darted quickly around. The timbre of his voice rose. He sounded sped up, using a lot of words in a long sentence that didn't end. I noticed that he was describing not actual problems in his present life but his reactions to what he perceived to be going on.

In this case, I was there to clutter bust not an object or a bunch of stuff but a habit that wasn't serving my client. So I stopped him. I asked him to breathe, and he took a deep breath. I asked him if he was comfortable in his chair. He moved his body around to get the right fit. I didn't say anything. I wanted to slow things down for him so he could see more clearly and find a solution. Finally, he seemed more centered. His eyes stopped moving around, and his focus was on the room.

He explained that he was panicking because he and his girlfriend were approaching their one-year anniversary of being together, and that was unusual for him. He was used to dating a lot of women and having turbulent relationships.

Part of him expected turbulence with his girlfriend, but they actually got along well.

He said, "I'm not used to things being easy. Isn't that weird? I'm uncomfortable with something good." He laughed.

I asked him how he felt about the woman he was flirting with online. He said, "She made me feel powerful when I was feeling uncomfortable with being vulnerable and softer with my girlfriend. It never felt good, though. It left me feeling like crap. I don't want to go there anymore."

It's easy to get distracted from feeling softer because we're not used to it. We tend to think it's unsafe. But if we try to escape these feelings, we lose much of the tender part of life, and this makes us feel sad and unfulfilled. We are actually less safe because we're not connected to ourselves. We're less aware. We look for other things to bring us satisfaction, but none of them feel as wonderful as our own gentle selves.

Busyness as a Buffer

My client had a fairly high-level job working for a television production company. But she didn't feel comfortable with herself, either in her job or at home. Her desk, floors, couch, and bookshelves were filled with random stuff. I had to take things off a chair to sit down. She was distracted and disconnected. It seemed like she was trying to amp herself up on coffee, talking about problems, or going off on rants as a way to cover up her deep exhaustion.

She told me she was married and had two kids, but she didn't see her family much because of the many hours she spent at her job. Her family often told her they missed her and wanted to spend more time with her. But her job was just too demanding, and so she ended up buying them expensive presents to make up for her guilt and their unhappiness. I could feel the deep sorrow in her heart.

Her family was sending her a powerful message: they felt separated from her. And she missed and felt disconnected from them too, but she couldn't let go of her job. In fact, she spent more time there than ever, and I sensed that the unmanageable clutter I'd been asked to help bust was actually the buffer she was using to paper over this conflict. The situation had almost completely worn her out.

I noticed a big poster from a Steven Spielberg movie on the wall. I asked her, "Do you like the poster?" She let out a big sigh. She said she wanted to be like Spielberg. She had devoted her life to reaching his level of filmmaking. But she sounded absent from her words. I said, "Would you buy this poster if you were out shopping today?" She paused. I sensed that she was feeling some emotional pain. Then she whispered, "No." She seemed surprised at her response. She felt present and strong for the first time.

I took the poster off the wall and took it out of its frame, handing it to her. She tore it up and put it in the trash. She sat there, stunned.

In that moment, being like Spielberg no longer served her. In fact, her attempts were causing both her and her family great pain, but she didn't fully recognize this because her career goals seemed so important. The busyness of life can, for a while, protect us from feeling fragile, hurt, and sorrowful. But we have to stay busy constantly to hold those feelings at bay. That's why we don't see that our busyness is also hurting us. We just end up thinking we must need more protection, more busyness. But we can only take so much before we start to break down.

She sat quietly. The spell had been broken. She looked like an actual person again; she was free. My client said, "Oh, my God, I can't work there anymore." Her voice had fullness and vitality. In that moment, she decided to quit her job. She called her husband to let him know of her decision. Her voice was filled with glee.

Later she told me that she had started a business that allowed her to work out of her home and for fewer hours. I spoke to her again recently. She said, "It's been a real adjustment from where I was to get here, but I am much happier overall. And so is my family. I've had most of my focus on my family for this past year, and it's been *wonderful*!"

EXERCISE

Relax and close your eyes. Mentally scan your body. Look for edginess. Find any places in your body that are tense or irritable. This is where some emotional clutter lives. You've knocked at its door, and it has answered.

Have a talk with the agitated sensation that lives at this address in your body. Introduce yourself. Tell it you were out for a stroll and thought you would drop in. Casualness is good. Ask how things are going. Be curious about what lives at this address in your body. There's a guest in your home: make the feelings welcome and safe, comfortable, so you can get to know each other.

Keep talking; engage in a discussion. Bring kindness into the part of your body that hasn't seen a friendly face in a while, and see what happens.

Coming Back to the Present

The reason lion tamers in the circus use a stool to keep a lion at bay is that the legs of the stool distract the lion. The animal's attention keeps focusing on the wooden legs and not on the delicious person holding the stool.

Like the lion, we're easily distracted from the present by our clutter. When there's more than one thing vying for our attention, we get caught up in those things and lose our connection with ourselves and others. Not much gets done. Attacking the stool seems like what we're supposed to do; quite often, we consider it our "job." This is the activity that we think makes us valuable. But as with my TV producer client, this overinvolvement only takes us away from what matters: the present.

Once I was working with a client who got a text message she said she had to reply to. I could feel her starting to get frantic as she typed away. When she came back to our clutter busting, less of her was present. Then a return text came in. She mumbled something, turned away, and started typing again. She looked agitated. When she was done, she looked around the room at the piles and boxes and said she didn't know if she could keep clutter busting.

Before the distractions came in, she had had a good flow going. She had gotten into the groove of considering just one thing at a time. She was open and connected to her sensitivity. But once she let other things capture her attention, she lost her focus and purpose and returned to her usual overwhelmed-by-everything state. Her attention was ricocheting off every item in the room.

I described to her what I saw happening. I told her that when we surround ourselves with things that don't serve us, our attention bounces off everything like a pinball. We get caught up in everything but the present moment, and this exhausts us. Noticing this dynamic when it happens is the first step to coming back to the present.

My client turned off her phone. We got back to clutter busting, and her attention was sharp and focused.

My clutter busts always come from the present moment. I help my clients ask themselves, "How do I feel right now? Not yesterday or last year, not how do I hope to feel tomorrow, but right now: Is this object helping me or causing me pain? If I'm feeling pain, what do I need to let go of to restore my connection with myself and others in this moment?" Anything that distracts us from seeing and feeling clearly in the present is clutter.

To use an example from my own life, at one point I was feeling amped up and unsatisfied in my cluttered thoughts about the things I was doing and the things I needed to do. I was tired and had lost my connection. In fact, I was so disconnected I didn't even know I was disconnected. I went over to my sister's house to pick up something. The only one home was her dog, Oliver, who was very happy to see me. He stood up on his hind legs and reached for me with his front paws. I forgot about all the stuff that had been prominent in my mind. I was happy again.

I took Oliver for a walk and realized that my mind's overinvolvement had been using me up. I'd mistaken all my mental hyperactivity for some kind of useful accomplishment, as if it had some value. Meanwhile, this cluttered thinking had exhausted me, which meant the work I was doing wasn't very good. But then in an instant, I reconnected with myself and my sense of pleasure in the moment. My true nature got a chance to shine.

When things clear and the connection returns, we stop loathing ourselves. That's the power of the present.

Fear as a Buffer

I've been performing stand-up comedy for twenty years. I'd thought about doing it for a year and a half before I ever made it onstage. I'd write lots of material, and I'd get the schedules and addresses of open-mike nights, but I was too intimidated to actually perform for an audience. I thought no one would laugh at the jokes I found funny. Sometimes I would find the courage to drive to a comedy club, but when I got there I'd stay in my car. I was too afraid to even go into the club.

Finally, one day I just did it. I drove to the club, went

inside, and signed up. I had to wait three hours before it was my turn onstage. I was so nervous! The four comics before me had the audience crying with laughter. The person before me was a Korean guy dressed like Elvis. He yelled, sang, and danced. He left the stage to huge applause.

Then it was my turn. I have a quiet personality, and I stood still and whispered my funny stories into the microphone. No one laughed. It was so quiet I could hear someone shift in their chair. I remember hearing the air-conditioning kick on. At one point I listened to the silence and thought how bizarre and exciting it was to stand in a club with a lot of people looking at me with no one making a sound.

A few minutes into my set I started to relax. I got it that no one was going to laugh, so I felt I had nothing to lose. I enjoyed performing what I had written. I thought it was funny and entertaining. I realized I wasn't like other comics, so people probably didn't know what to make of me. I left the stage to a few claps. One guy in the audience stopped me and said, "What kind of acid are you on?" I went to my car and drove home happy.

I realized during the car ride home that my year and a half of worrying about what people would think of me as a comic was just a buffer because it kept me from connecting with others in my unique way. When I actually got onstage and performed, I was afraid, but I had a good time. I was exposed and unprotected, and yet *I felt safe*. The experience was amazing. I found value not in the protection but in actively, honestly connecting with myself in front of other people.

Make two cups of tea. Set one cup down on a table. Place the other cup just across from it. Have a seat before one cup. Take a sip.

Imagine that your fear is sitting by the other cup of tea. It's a kind gesture to offer some tea to your fear. Take another sip of tea. Introduce yourself. Imagine that your fear introduces itself. Ask your fear what it's been up to. Be curious about what it's been doing. What does fear do with its day? Where does it like to show up in your life?

Tell fear what you've been up to when it's not around. Fear's curious too. It wants to know what you do when it's somewhere else. Ask fear what it likes best about being part of you. What does it like least? Does fear always enjoy its job? Be curious about its answers. Ask yourself, "I wonder what it's like to be fear?"

When you're done, thank fear for talking with you. Tell it you appreciate its work on your behalf. Promise your fear that you'll always listen to and respect it when it helps you. But remind it that you don't always need it. If there are any jobs fear doesn't enjoy, tell your fear it doesn't need to do them anymore. You'll manage without it. Then promise to have tea with your fear again later. Everyone likes a nice chat.

– Everything
is pretty
gentle until
it's put on
a leash.

Chapter Four

THE URGE TO CHANGE OTHERS

Sometimes we are more eager to fix someone else's clutter than our own. Someone does or has something that bothers us, and we think they should do it differently or get rid of that thing. So we tell them what we think. We point out their clutter. Perhaps we are only voicing our frustration, or perhaps we genuinely feel that the other person will be enlightened by our words and make the change. But then they don't do what we suggest. They like things the way they are. To them, their actions or possessions aren't clutter. Their reaction bothers us.

When we are upset about someone else's clutter, those feelings become our clutter. When two people hold fast to their position of being right, seeing the other person as wrong, they've created clutter in their relationship. Both people become irritated and upset, and the relationship suffers.

Fishing Bobbers

I saw this type of conflict in action with a couple at a clutter-busting seminar. The husband was talking about his collection of fishing bobbers (small floats used to suspend the lure when fishing). He had more than twelve hundred of them. His wife, who was sitting next to him, spoke up, saying that she didn't like them. She felt they were clutter that he needed to get rid of. The wife was angry. She had her arms crossed and refused to look at him. Then she admitted that she had thrown out some of the bobbers when he wasn't looking. He said that he wanted her to be okay with his keeping the bobbers. She reiterated that she wanted him to get rid of them. They said they'd been arguing over this for fifteen years!

I could tell that both partners wanted me to exonerate them. Each wanted me to say they were right and the other was wrong. They reminded me of countries that had been at war for many years.

I said that neither of them was going to change. They had strong convictions about how things should be, and they expected the other to hear what they wanted and to change. But their experience showed that wasn't going to happen. I told them that the best thing they could do was just accept what the other wanted. They didn't have to take any particular action, just accept that the other person was making a request.

The couple didn't want to hear this and started in on each other again. They each winced at the other's angry and violent words. I sensed that their anger was motivated by a fear of being hurt. If they opened up and accepted the other, they would be exposing their soft underbellies, and that must have terrified them. The sadness in their eyes and voices made it obvious they were suffering.

What I see again and again when I clutter bust with roommates, partners, or spouses is that when we try to make the other person feel bad about what they want, we are actually punishing our relationship. The real clutter wasn't this couple's bobbers — it was their habit of hiding from each other behind the armor of control.

I asked if they liked each other. They each said yes and looked at each other with shy love. Then, I said, it was worth recognizing the toll their long-running fight was taking on their relationship and how much it must be hurting their hearts. Their derision toward each other was hurting their relationship more than the bobbers were.

A relationship is a living thing. Whether it's with a partner, friend, family member, or coworker, a relationship is tangible. Since we want our relationships to serve and support us, we want to be kind to them. It's worth treating the relationships in our lives as entities to be cared for. Coming from this perspective, I told the couple that when they were driving home after the talk, or when they were lying in bed that night or the next morning, they could talk about how they could best come to terms with the situation. They could talk about how they could live with things as they were and be happy.

I could see in their eyes that they were caught off guard by this interpretation of what was happening. They didn't have any words to counter what I said to them, and they couldn't continue their fight. They were aware of the damage their long-standing fight was having on their relationship, and they couldn't put their armor back on. They were reconnected.

There's vitality when two people drop their defenses and reconnect. It opens their hearts. With an open awareness, they refocus on maintaining the satisfying parts of their relationship. Seeing a relationship as a living entity gives us the courage to treat it with kindness.

Dolls versus Guitars

Here's an example of a similar dynamic, in which both parties wanted to change the other without changing the relationship — but with a twist. I was giving a clutter-busting talk when a man in the audience raised his hand. He asked, "What about collections? Are they clutter?"

I could tell by his tone that he felt collections *were* clutter, and since the woman sitting next to him was wincing and had her arms crossed over her chest, I knew he was talking about her collections.

Sure enough, when I asked him, "Whose collections are you talking about?" he said, "My wife's." People in the room laughed. They related to being bothered by other people's stuff. But there was also something deeper: I think they all recognized the desire to change someone else. We've all been on both sides of the situation. We know from experience that we hate being told what to do. And yet we've all tried to tell someone else what to do, only to be frustrated by their resistance.

I said to her, "I'm guessing you're his wife?" She nodded. Anger flared in her eyes.

He said, "She's got this porcelain doll collection. I
don't like it. It takes up so much space in the living room
that we can't entertain people. I don't understand why she
has to have them."

She said, "The dolls aren't a problem. I like them. They
aren't clutter. He needs to stop yapping about them....
His guitars, they're the problem. They take up so much
space that we can't have people over and entertain in the
basement."

Each of them thought the problem was the other person's stuff. Each thought that if the other person changed,
they'd feel better. But trying to change someone else, telling
them what they *should* do, creates a break in the relationship.
We've blamed someone else for our own uncomfortable
emotions, and they resent it and resist. If we push harder,
thinking we'll force them to change, the pain increases. It

becomes difficult to be together. And it will remain this way until we see the problem for what it is: our own discomfort with and resistance to things the way they are.

I asked the couple to stop talking about it. In these kinds of situations, I like to help the couple acknowledge what the other person is saying. Couples often don't hear each other because they are too busy trying to defend themselves.

I pointed out that the woman likes her dolls. Her husband doesn't like them. She's going to keep the dolls no matter what he says. She doesn't like his guitar collection. The husband likes his guitars. He's going to keep them no matter what she says. When clutter busting, this is what people really need to hear: *you can't make another person get rid of their things*. No one likes to be told what to do, and nagging never makes someone do what you want them to do. I'll say it again: Trying to change another person is itself clutter. It hurts the relationship.

Yes, you *can* find another person difficult, and in time you can choose to leave that person if necessary (more on this in chapter 7). But your life is going to be so much easier when you don't try to change them.

At the workshop, the couple again started in on each other about their things. I butted in and said, "That's the clutter I'm talking about." They were so used to their argument that they didn't notice the hold it had on them. "You can't complain about each other this way anymore. It's detrimental to your peace of mind and to the health of your relationship. Seriously, you'll be a lot happier if you toss the argument and agree that you each have things the other doesn't like...and recognize that *you like each other.*" I wanted to point out that liking each other is something they have in common.

They went quiet. They understood that I was asking them to consider their relationship rather than just the dolls and guitars. After a pause, they agreed that they were lucky to have each other in their lives and they didn't want to step on their relationship anymore.

The unity we feel with ourselves and with others is the most satisfying and fulfilling experience possible. When fear or anger shatters this experience, we lose something precious. It helps to stop and notice our loss. Is it worth the loss to gain control? If not, we must do what we can to reclaim the connection.

EXERCISE

Sometimes we don't like someone's actions. It's natural to feel that way. But when not liking becomes feeling that the other person is wrong, we suffer. We become wrapped up in their actions, and we lose our peace of mind.

Here's an exercise to help unravel the pain and misery of this situation.

- Think of someone you are at odds with. They are doing something you don't like, and it's driving you crazy.

- Feel the strain this is creating in your body and mind. See the details of the anguish. What kinds of thoughts has this been producing in you? How does thinking and feeling this way affect your body? Imagine how much energy it takes to maintain this disturbance. In what ways does this run you down?

- Remember: Don't look at what this person has said and done. Just examine your reactions.

- Now imagine observing yourself from the outside, as a third person. What reactions do you see yourself having? As an observer, how does seeing them make you feel? Do you want to say anything to yourself? If so, go ahead.

- Return to yourself and your feeling of injustice. Do you want to continue experiencing the effects of these emotions on your body and mind? You can if you want. You're good at holding on to them. Since the other person is going to stay as they are, what would best serve you?

- I heard it said once that resentment is like drinking poison and expecting the other person to die. Do your feelings about the other person serve you, or do you want to let those feelings go?

The Ugly, Comfortable Couch

Sometimes a person gets tremendous pleasure from an object that we detest. Just seeing the thing rubs us the wrong way. We feel that we can't be happy until the person gets rid of the thing — basically, until they change their behavior. So we let them know our feelings. But the other person likes the object and wants to keep it. If we stay stuck in our revulsion while they hang on to what they love, the relationship suffers.

One of my blog readers wrote me about one such situation:

> *Here's a couch dilemma for you, Brooks. So, hubby and I have been married for twenty-five years now. And for twenty-five years I have been suffering with a couch that I cannot stand, but, yeah, you guessed it — he LOVES! Why does he love such an albatross? He says it's the only couch he's ever found that he can lie end to end on comfortably. I've tried three unsuccessful times to introduce new (used) couches, and all three times, no go. Argh! I even considered recovering the cushions, even bought nice fabric to do so. In the end, I just couldn't bring myself to spend the time to make something nice for a piece of furniture I abhorred, especially when I knew the nice cushion covers would likely end up all snagged due to all the stuff attached to his belt. Brooks, what's a gal to do? We are on an extremely tight budget. It seems awful to deny*

*my hubby his ugly couch, but it's definitely affecting
ME. Do I change my outlook on it? If so, HOW?*

I wrote to her that it was obvious her husband loves and enjoys his couch. It's rare for him to find a piece of furniture he feels physically comfortable on, and he doesn't want to let it go. She can't understand how he could feel this way, asking, "Why does he love such an albatross?" The thing is, he loves it. That's the important thing. That's what is. Instead of being caught up with thinking that he shouldn't feel this way, she could instead choose to be happy that he has a couch he enjoys so much.

Maybe she thinks it's still possible to get him to change his mind. But after twenty-five years, he hasn't. Acceptance of what is, when it can't be changed, gives us peace of mind. It's when we think things shouldn't be the way they are that we suffer. After reading my note, she wrote back:

Thanks, Brooks, for the reality check. Gulp. Hard to hear, but easy to understand. Hubby and I have compromised on finding a more attractive cover for it. I can live with that. He also has agreed to fix the broken spring and be the keeper of the falling cushions. Sounds like a win-win to me. Thanks too for bringing some sanity and cooperation back to this issue.

This woman's extreme discomfort with her husband's couch wasn't serving her, and when she saw that, she negotiated a compromise. Sometimes all it takes is seeing we've gone too far. We can say to ourselves, "This is hurting me and the relationship, and nothing is getting better."

But if we can't drop our obsession with another's possessions, we need to look within and ask, "What's going on? Is there something that I need that I'm not taking care of?" Perhaps the other person's joy reminds us that we also need some tending and care. Perhaps we fear the other loves the object more than us.

We're complex creatures. Our actions often don't make apparent sense. It helps to humbly recognize this and be patient with ourselves as we look at what's going on under the surface.

EXERCISE

Sometimes we love doing or owning something that a person we are close to abhors. They let us know they hate it and may even try to convince us to drop this activity or thing.

In this exercise, take a minute and ask yourself: "Is a parent, child, spouse, friend, or business associate currently objecting to anything I do or own?"

In the same way that we can be uncomfortable with something someone else owns or does, others may sometimes feel the same way about things we own or do. We can't be close to others and not feel this way.

Now close your eyes and honestly ask yourself these questions:

- Can I allow others not to like a particular
  thing I own or do?
- Can I accept another's feelings in the same
  way I would want them to accept my feelings
  about their things?
- What can I do that would allow openness to
  take over this situation?

Open your eyes and write down everything
you can think of that would help restore your connection. Start with, "Let go of being right."

The Power of Listening

When we stop listening to the other person in a relationship, we're no longer in relationship with them. We are by
ourselves in a room with another person. This has a way of
hurting the other person, and they react accordingly. There
are now two hurt people reactively talking at each other,
often using unkind words, trying to make the other do what
they want them to do.

I was working with a couple who were getting along
pretty well until I came upon a large stack of fancy shopping bags. There were probably more than a hundred.
The wife was confused about what to do with them. The

husband stopped listening and became critical of his wife, saying angrily, "Why don't you get rid of them? You don't need them!" She shrank back and looked ashamed. He said, "Seriously, it's stupid of you to hang on to these bags!" She replied, "Don't tell me what to do. I'm keeping them." He looked at me and said, "Can you talk with her and help her see that this stuff is clutter!" She brooded and sighed. He said to her, "Seriously, honey, snap out of it —"

I said to him, "Don't say anything more."

I turned to the woman and said in a gentle voice, "How many of these bags do you think you need?"

She softened, her defensive tension melting away. She thought about it and said, "Um, I don't know — maybe five."

I said, "Okay, let's pick your five favorites." She did. I put the ones she didn't pick in the recycling bin. Her husband's mouth was hanging open. To him, what I'd done seemed like a miracle.

I said, "This is the way to talk to your wife. It helps when you listen to her."

This was a classic situation in which one person's unwillingness to listen was the reason a clutter problem wasn't being resolved. Further, the husband's expressions of anger and frustration were far more damaging than a pile of unnecessary bags.

We can't berate people into action. They'll resent us. Then all parties involved are receiving less love and feeling hurt. When we speak with kindness, and listen with compassion, our relationship will thank us.

Chapter Five

HOW TO QUIET
THE CLUTTER STORMS

You're getting along with your spouse. There's a nice flow between the two of you. Then suddenly you are triggered by an object or something your spouse does, and the unity is broken. The peace of mind you'd been feeling is replaced with anger and a deep sense of injustice. You think, "What is this *doing* here? It shouldn't *be* here!" or "They shouldn't have done this! It's not fair!" It feels like an emotional thunderstorm inside, and you feel compelled to right the wrong.

Some objects, and situations, are loaded with significance. We don't see them coming, and then — BOOM! — they set off emotional land mines inside us. We react with great intensity toward the other person. Where do these emotions come from?

These strong reactions indicate the presence of emotional clutter in our relationships. We need to recognize these spasms when they occur, or we get lost in the feelings and act from a state of confusion. Typically, either we become defensive or we go on the attack, and a vicious argument ensues. Each hurts the other with words and actions. Deep down both people are trying to protect themselves from being hurt, and both are doing what they can to defend themselves.

Our fights over stuff are clutter. Our emotional reactions to things destroy the sense of unity and connection in our relationships and almost always make matters worse. It's hard to see or anticipate this clutter until we find ourselves in the midst of it, and then, in all the tumult, it's easy to forget that our emotions are the clutter we need to bust. Our passion and righteousness sweep us up, like a mob against an oppressor. Only later do we wonder about and perhaps regret what happened. We ask, "Where did that come from? Why did I say those things? How come I couldn't control myself?"

When these storms happen, if we approach them with awareness, we can actually use them to help us identify and clean up our relationship clutter. This chapter is devoted to helping you use your awareness to break the clutter cycles in your relationships.

Stench under the Bed

I was working with a couple in their bedroom. They were being kind to each other until I asked them about the large rug under their bed. The man said it had been passed down to him from his great-grandmother. The woman said she didn't like it and accused him of putting his family before her. Immediately, they started yelling at each other, saying personal, accusatory, and vicious things. Then it got down to basics when she said he never supported her in what she wanted to do. He said she never felt he was good enough. Their words and tone were so violent, it felt as if they were hitting each other with full swings to the gut. I tried to get them to stop, but they wouldn't.

An interesting thing about this couple is that they had rabbits that ran loose around their condo. They had concrete floors, which made it easy to clean up the rabbits' mess. During their argument, one of the rabbits ran under the bed. I stuck my head under the bed and was hit with an intense odor. The rug, the spark for the argument, was soaked entirely in rabbit pee. It was also covered with hundreds of rabbit poops. I quickly stood back up.

I stood between the couple and told them to stop fighting. They were screaming so loudly, I had to yell, and even then they didn't hear me at first. Finally they did. They were filled with adrenaline and fury, and at the same time they looked emotionally spent and damaged. I said they couldn't yell at each other like that. They were tearing holes in each other's hearts as well as in their own, and it wasn't making them feel better. It was moving them further and further away from each other. They were both hurting, and they wanted the pain in their hearts to stop. I told them that we all want to feel good, but that using violence toward another won't stop the pain we are feeling inside. They'd been so caught up in the rage they felt toward each other that they didn't realize they were sleeping over filth.

I said, "The carpet under your bed is filled with rabbit piss and shit. That's what things have come to. This violent hatred isn't serving you, and this is the proof."

The argument-induced haze cleared, and they got down and looked under the bed. They couldn't believe it had gotten so bad and that they hadn't noticed. They looked at each other without saying a word. They were equally embarrassed and connected.

They agreed that the rug was beyond saving. They lifted the bed, and I pulled out the rug. I cut it up and put the pieces in garbage bags and brought it outside to the trash. When I got back, they were mopping the floor under the bed. The couple were silent. Their awareness had been split wide open. They seemed so much more alive. They were beautiful creatures without their armor. They were feeling so much, and now they weren't trying to stop the feelings.

It's impossible for us to clean up our shared spaces without finding the emotional clutter we've hidden there. When it reveals itself, we can either fight about it or confront and resolve the problem. We can mop up the shit!

Emotional Tornados

As you become aware of the emotional tornado erupting inside, recognize it for what it is: a psychological cataclysmic event in which your emotions and thoughts are tightly clenched. The experience can't be halted immediately. But by being aware of what's happening, you can resist taking action or lashing out — you can wait until the tantrum ends. It's useful to wait, even if you don't want to. Your emotions may sound like a trumpet calling you to war, but there's no war. But if you act on the call, you may very well start one. It's okay just to feel these emotions without acting on them. You've touched a place where your connection with another has been broken, and it hurts.

Assigning blame, whether we are blaming the other person or ourselves for our pain, doesn't help reestablish our connection. Blame is clutter and doesn't serve us. What helps us reconnect is recognizing our inner emotional tornado. It has a life of its own, and it's taken hold of us.

Wait for the storm to pass, even if it seems to take forever. You might want to confront your partner; yell at your kid; tell your boss where she can shove your job; break something; hurt someone. But as the emotions ebb, the reactive urge will eventually be replaced by a deep and profound calm. That's the return of connection — both with yourself and with the other person.

Reconnecting is the only way to feel better.

Window Blinds

I was hired by a couple to help them clutter bust their condo. As we progressed I began sensing some tension. They seemed to be avoiding contact with each other.

When working with them in their bedroom, I noticed some fabric on a cardboard tube in the closet. Though it looked insignificant, it felt meaningful in some way. When I asked about it, I could feel the tension between them rise. The wife sheepishly said, "It's fabric." I said, "What's it for?" She didn't answer. In a hushed, angry tone the husband said, "It's to make blinds for the window. The streetlights are right outside our window, and they keep me up at night. My wife said she would make the blinds three years ago, and she hasn't done it yet." She looked down and gritted her teeth.

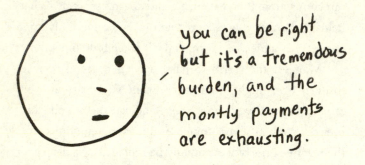

you can be right but it's a tremendous burden, and the montly payments are exhausting.

I said to her, "Is that so?" She said, "Yes." I said, "How come you haven't been able to get to them?" She angrily glanced at her husband and looked away. She said, "Because I've been busy taking care of our daughter."

I said, "How long would it take to make them?" She said, "About five hours." Neither of them said anything. They wouldn't look at each other. I could see that they were both dug into their anger.

The fabric roll may have been hidden in the closet, out of sight, but it hadn't been forgotten. Neither had let go of their mounting hurts over the unfinished task, and their disconnection had grown. They blamed each other for their hurt feelings, built up their defenses, and became involved in their anguish. It felt like they were no longer in relationship with each other. Instead they were invested in holding on to their pain.

In situations like this, I find it helps to just say what's true, without judgment and even without the goal of changing anything. So I put the fabric roll on the bed. I said to the husband that he was angry with his wife because she said she would make the blinds three years ago and hadn't done it. He agreed. I said to the wife that she had said she would do it, but she'd been too busy to get to them, and she was feeling hurt by her husband's anger. She agreed.

I asked if she could hire someone to make the blinds. She relaxed and said she hadn't thought about that. I suggested that she place an ad on Craigslist and look at the responses and go with the one that seemed best. I told both of them that if the fabric roll remained in their bedroom closet, the husband would keep getting angrier, and the wife would remain resentful and guilty. Their combined anger and resistance would destroy their marriage, peace of mind, and health. Trying to hide the issue in their closet hadn't lessened its impact.

Things don't start out in disconnection. With this couple, his request for blinds and her offer to make them were both probably made in good faith. But sometimes things slip. We get busy, overwhelmed, and tired. Or maybe we use our actions to say something we feel we can't say with words. Whatever the reason, if we don't talk about what's going on, it's easy for misunderstandings to grow. Our anger builds in us and grows louder. Maybe we hope that the other person will just know what we're feeling and make the change we want. Perhaps the other person is feeling the same way.

But resentful silence is not communication. The only way to reconnect is to drop the armor of angry silence and risk being open again. Say what your experience is and ask what you can do to make things better. I gently started the process with this couple, redirecting them to a new solution.

The couple agreed to hire someone to make the blinds. Suddenly, there was a strong feeling of peace in the room, which surprised them. They each felt heard. Their connection was restored.

The Stash

Sometimes when I clutter bust with a couple, we find things that surprise one of them. Maybe it's something from a previous relationship, something that was supposed to have been thrown away, or something they simply didn't know the other possessed. It touches a nerve and accusations fly: one feels hurt, the other defensive. Each protects themselves by claiming to be right. Then they fight over who's right rather than addressing the real source of pain.

I once worked with a couple in their home office. The husband left the room for a minute to take a call, and I was going through the closet with the wife. We came upon a box of the husband's *Sports Illustrated* swimsuit issues. She was surprised at first, and then she looked very sad. Then her eyes filled with rage and she began to shake. I could tell she was fuming inside.

She yelled to the other room, "I found your bikini magazines! I want them out of here now!" He got off the phone and came into the room, saying, "I'm not getting rid of those. You can't tell me what to do!" She started crying and said, "Why are you doing this to me?" He said, "What? Why are you saying that? I'm not doing anything!" I stepped in and told the husband that his wife's feelings were hurt. She wasn't actually angry with him, despite her tone. Sometimes when we feel hurt it comes out as anger. It's a way of protecting ourselves when we are feeling vulnerable. I told the wife that her husband was reacting to her anger. Someone's anger can catch us by surprise and make us feel afraid. It's hard to admit to being afraid, since that's being vulnerable too.

She opened up and said that when she saw the magazines she felt sad that she was no longer young, and she felt that her husband didn't care for her. He apologized for making her feel that way. He grew softer as he said that what she felt wasn't true. He thought she was beautiful, and he felt sad that she thought he didn't love her anymore.

EXERCISE

As you saw in each of the stories in this chapter, I took very similar steps to calm the storm. Since

I won't be in your living room, how can you do this for yourself when a storm erupts? Just follow these steps:

1. When you become aware that you're in the midst of an emotional clutter storm with another person, stop what you are doing. Don't do anything for a few seconds.

2. Both of you want to be heard, and no one is listening. Begin to listen to the other person. Now repeat back what the other person is telling you. You're not saying that they're right or agreeing with them. You're confirming that you're really listening to the other person by repeating what you've heard: "You're saying you feel/want _____." Notice your tone of voice. If it's harsh, repeat your statement in a neutral, compassionate voice. Once you make that emotional switch, you have started to reconnect. Now listen to the other's response.

3. Stop. Don't say anything for a few seconds. The space of silence gives both of you a chance to realign with yourselves and each other. Plus, it allows the adrenaline to diminish.

4. Then tell the person how you feel, as in, "I'm angry because I feel afraid that..." Listen to your tone of voice. If it's defensive or angry,

keep repeating your perspective until you can do so in a compassionate or neutral way.

5. Continue this process until the connection is complete.

If at any time during this process you come to feel that you are working hard while the other person isn't, even though you are the one who's right — that's clutter. Someone has to break the cycle, and in this moment, that's you.

Being Heard

I once clutter busted with seven members of a family who were arguing with one another over almost every decision. One person would want to let go of or hang on to something, while another attacked their choice. The attack would make the first person become defensive. The room had an explosive feeling.

There was something going on under the surface that was more powerful than words. I felt that, essentially, everyone wanted a chance to be noticed, to feel they mattered. It had probably been a long while since they felt heard by one another. Living that way generates a lot of hurt. Getting caught up in clutter, in the things that don't matter to our hearts, keeps us closed off to our feelings and our connections with others. This takes a toll on us because we need to feel openness and connection to experience well-being.

I wanted to help each member of the family feel safe by making sure they felt heard. When one of the family members got angry about another's choice, and received a defensive response, I repeated back both of their positions. I stated each position with compassion because I wanted to echo each person's needs with openness. I wanted to encourage the family's underlying desire to connect. Each time two people heard what they wanted spoken back to them, they became quieter and softer.

As each family member felt they were being heard, the arguments over things lessened, as did the loud barks of defensiveness and anger. They began enjoying one another's company. They became supportive.

It doesn't matter what we keep or throw away if, when we're done, everyone feels heard and respected and connected to one another. The funny thing is, in that kind of supportive atmosphere, people loosen their grip on their things and are more open to recognizing what's no longer important to them.

Locked Horns

I overheard a man telling his wife about two deer he had found frozen to death in a lake. They had fallen through the ice. Since their antlers were locked, it appears they had been fighting on the frozen lake and the ice had given way. Because they were locked in battle, they couldn't save themselves and they froze to death.

This is how I sometimes find couples when I come to clutter bust their homes. They are emotionally stuck, frozen together in locked positions; their relationship is drowning, but they won't let go and step back because they are too afraid of being hurt. They are no longer protecting and caring for each other; they are trying to coerce, control, or change them. Winning seems imperative for their own well-being and safety. Love has left the room.

Awareness, seeing what's actually happening, is very powerful. Mutual recognition that we have locked horns, that anger and fear have taken over, is sometimes all that's needed to calm down, stop fighting, and focus on finding a solution that heals our connection.

It starts with the recognition of the compulsive habit of seeking false self-protection. We fear being hurt, and we want to hide our vulnerability. So we put on the armor of emotional defenses, but this interrupts our connection with those we love. The other person can feel hurt by our efforts, and they become defensive in turn. Fear takes over, and we get tangled up in each other's innocent attempts at trying to stay safe.

Sometimes these battles have been going on for years; at other times, it is as if we have been ambushed by our fears, and we react instantaneously to protect ourselves. The key is being able to recognize whether or not we are in any actual danger when we are getting defensive and putting on our armor.

If we're lucky, we notice the initial budding of our control clutter so we can drop it before much damage has been done. The telltale signs of this kind of clutter are often physiological. There's the immediate heat of anxiety in our bloodstreams. This is an alarm telling us that something is wrong and we are in danger. But is there actual danger? Is a car heading toward us? Or is the danger an emotional phantasmagoria?

Human beings are strange. We can get scared of shadows in the dark. It's easy for us to see things that aren't actually there. Our imagination often blends with our perception of what we think is reality. Mix in our unconscious fears, tiredness, and low blood sugar, and you're going to have misunderstandings. I've certainly thought the worst of someone I loved when all I needed was a snack and a nap.

If we don't notice our initial call to battle, and we lock horns with another, we might realize in the midst of our fury that we've been overtaken by our fear of being hurt. Something triggered us — it's not necessary to know what — and we recognize that we are now at extreme odds with someone we care about. We are attacking someone we would usually protect from being attacked. Recognizing that we would normally protect this person can take the adrenaline out of our need to intensely defend ourselves.

Maybe the other person is still intent on maintaining their defensive reactions. But now we can see that they are motivated by fear, as we were a few seconds ago. Knowing that their reaction is not personal can allow us to open up and listen. This can create a crack in the person's armor that can let the light through.

The effect can be so sudden it's almost surreal. A couple I worked with were having a vicious argument in their living room. One man was trying to make the other get rid of most of his DVD collection. He chastised his partner for having so many DVDs. He delighted in pointing out that his partner never watched all the movies he bought, that it wasted money and took up too much space. The partner defended his right to have the films and began attacking the other for his numerous books. He said he felt like they were living in a stuffy library. I could tell that, whatever they were fighting about, it had nothing to do with DVDs and books.

Suddenly one of the partners shifted. The furious heat left his body. The other partner was still angry but noticed the shift and fell silent. For several long moments, the only sound was their breathing. The storm was over. They apologized to each other. They were a couple again.

EXERCISE

This exercise is a clutter-busting exploration done between two people sharing a space. You'll be working hand in hand. No antlers in this one.

Explore your shared space, and consider your things as a team. Pick one thing at a time, and ask, "Does this serve us, or not?"

You want to avoid attacking or commenting on the other person for what they have to say. Stay curious about each other's answers. It helps to hear what your other half is feeling because it affects you as part of the whole.

Talk about resistance as it comes up. You can say, "When you said _____, I felt _____." Or, "When you say that you want to keep _____, I feel _____." Be curious and listen to each other. Repeat what the other person says so they know you hear how they're feeling. This encourages openness.

If you find things that you both feel don't serve you, remove them.

As you finish with each item, move on to the next and continue asking, "Does this serve us?"

Holding Hands

Sometimes couples get caught up in uncomfortable details of the moment and forget about the power of their connection. I worked with a couple who were feeling very stuck in their clutter. The woman talked about being so overwhelmed with her stuff that she couldn't move forward or even begin letting go. Her husband said that living with her clutter made him angry. He said that he didn't have much stuff, and he was frustrated that she couldn't live the same way.

They couldn't look each other in the eye. They looked away when they spoke. The woman was feeling a lot of shame. The man was mad. They'd been living this way for a long time.

I noticed that they were holding hands. Their grip was

tight and powerful. I asked the woman if she liked her man. Her heart opened, and she said yes. I asked the man if he liked her, and he passionately said yes. I pointed to the fact that they were holding hands. I said, "This is serving you. The connection between the two of you is powerful." I said it was obvious that they fed each other.

How they were feeling about their clutter situation was the actual clutter. When she felt shame for not being able to let go, she was separating herself from him. When he was angry at her stuckness, he broke their connection.

I said some part of her must have felt that the shame was serving her, that it was the means to change herself; otherwise, she wouldn't have continued feeling that way. He must have felt his constant anger would cause her to change. But neither shame nor anger can produce positive change.

I told them that the genuine article was their connection, that it brought them their greatest joy. They could strengthen that by stepping off the gas pedal of their shame and anger and figuring out a kinder way to help and encourage each other. I suggested that, if they took some time to gently clutter bust things together, it would bring them closer. Working together could increase the comfort they felt in their home.

One of the great things about letting go of what no longer serves us is that we become reacquainted with the things we love. The distractions are gone, and we're left with the things that actually nurture us. We appreciate the people we love because we can finally see them.

Chapter Six

CLUTTER BUSTING OLD RELATIONSHIPS

Just because a relationship ends, that doesn't mean it stops affecting us. People who were once part of our lives remain in our hearts and memories, as well as in the stuff they leave behind. Sometimes it's as if they are ghosts inhabiting the objects that remind us of them. These objects are clutter when they make us feel melancholy, regretful, fearful, or lethargic. When they remind us of our loss and pain, they can split us off from the things that matter to us now and can keep us from creating new, fulfilling relationships.

This chapter looks at the clutter we have acquired from people who have died, as well as from broken relationships, such as divorces and failed romances. We also have a relationship with past versions of ourselves, and I'll discuss how to know when it's time to clutter bust these as well.

Divorce: Removing the Shrapnel

Many of my clients' homes are affected by divorce. Either my clients are in the midst of divorce or they already have gone through one many years ago, and the fallout lingers in their living spaces. Divorce is painful, and so we often withdraw emotionally to protect ourselves. But this withdrawal prevents the openness we need in order to heal and feel love again. If we leave reminders of our pain lying around in the stuff we've hung on to from that relationship, it's as if we have left the shrapnel we received during a war in our bodies. We can't heal properly or completely because the wounds remain fresh. By removing and letting go of these sharp remnants, my clients find they feel safe enough to experience joy and love again.

I was helping my client, who was divorced, clutter bust the clothing in her closet. She had a pretty good letting-go momentum going until we came upon an oblong box on the top shelf. On was box was a label that said "My Wedding Dress." When I asked what she wanted to do with the dress, she looked pale and sickly, and her eyes were filled with sadness and fear. She said she didn't want to talk about it — she just wanted to leave it up on the shelf. I felt like a doctor examining a patient and coming across a great source of pain in the body. I took the box off the shelf and said, "Follow me."

I put the box on her bed and removed the lid. The wedding gown was visible under a plastic cover. We stood on opposite sides of the bed and looked down on it. It was as if we were looking down on a body.

I asked her again what she wanted to do with the dress, and she said she had to think about it. I could see a lot of emotions rising up in her. She was feeling fragile and vulnerable, and this scared her. As she tried to bring her emotions under control, she vacantly said she wanted her two daughters to have the option of wearing the dress when they got married.

I sensed this decision gave her more power — not her natural power, but a protective armor that shielded her tender self from being hurt. She looked very far away, like an empty shell. What was she really preserving, and for whom? Whatever was going on inside her, she was suddenly disconnected from herself.

I said, "Do you want your daughters to marry into the legacy of this dress? There's a lot of unhappiness associated with this outfit. You might want them to get a fresh start. It would be nice to let them choose the dress they would like to wear if they get married." She agreed, but she still seemed sad.

I said if she were to let go of the wedding dress and its sad associations, it would create a space for something new and supportive to come into her life. I told her that we all deserve to be happy, whether that means being happy by ourselves or happy with someone else who is kind to us.

She smiled and took a deep breath. The light came back into her eyes. I sensed the fatigue of living with this failed relationship slipping from her. She wanted to take better care of herself. She said she wanted to let go of the dress. I put it in the donate pile.

Sometimes we hold on to the broken pieces of a relationship because we've lost a connection with someone we once held dear and we feel a deep sadness. The person is gone from our life, and we want them back, or we want to remember how wonderful it was to be in love with them. A part of us lives as if we were still in relationship with the person. We are trying to keep the past alive in the present moment, and this creates conflict in our hearts.

This was the case for another client who was going through an intense divorce and child-custody battle. She seemed brittle and fearful. She looked down a lot. The world seemed to have become too much for her.

We were going through the boxes in her bedroom closet, and we came across a shiny, gold-colored box containing photos from her wedding ceremony. She said she didn't want to go through what was inside because it would be too painful. I suggested that I hand her a few photos at a time. She could take a quick look and see if she'd like to let them go. I gently reminded her that the box was worth going through because the presence in our homes of something that makes us feel bad always has a detrimental effect on us.

She agreed. It was slow going, since there were hundreds of photos. She was feeling a lot of anguish. In a quiet and broken voice she said, "I think I need to hang on to all these for my son to look at when he's older."

I sensed that she didn't really want to keep all those photos for her son. She was feeling overwhelmed and tremendously uncomfortable because of the pain of her loss.

To let go of these photos would be to admit her marriage was over. She would be letting go of the relationship. I knew that if the box of wedding photos went back in the closet, she probably would not go through them again. They would sit there like shrapnel embedded in her life and continue to negatively influence her and her son.

I said, "The thing you need to do for your son is to be happy now. He needs you to be strong, present, and open in his life. I suggest you keep the photos that will make you feel that way." She smiled and sat up. She quickly looked through and picked five photos and happily tossed the rest away.

Sometimes what we do to avoid pain only ends up expanding it. This pain ends up crippling us. When we compassionately accept that we are hurt in the moment, we give the pain a chance to run its course and fade away.

I had another client whose garage was affected by divorce clutter. She and her ex had split three years earlier, but half her garage was filled with his stuff. The space felt dark and heavy. She didn't even want to look at any of the things. I told her how depressed and weighed down she looked in the stuff's presence. I said that every time she pulled her car into the garage, seeing her ex's stuff negatively affected her. I added that the ghosts embodied by this stuff passed through the garage's walls and came into her living room and her heart. She didn't like this image, so she agreed to go through her ex's things.

Since most of the stuff in the boxes was his, I asked if she could contact him and ask him to come get his boxes.

She said his place was too small to house the stuff and that she didn't want to impose on him. I said that he was imposing on her. The presence of his stuff in her home was hurting and exhausting her, leaving her less available for her nine-year-old daughter.

Maybe, by keeping her ex's stuff, my client was punishing herself for divorcing him. Perhaps she thought she was being kind, holding on to his things so he would feel less hurt. If so, she was trying to manage his experience. Hanging on to his things was becoming the same as holding on to the marriage, and she was suffering as a result. She wouldn't be finally divorced until she gave all his stuff back.

I said to her, "You can't control this. Trying to make things better for him is hurting you. Let's call him and ask him to come and get his things."

She called him and made her request. He resisted taking his things back. But she insisted. They agreed that he would come over and get his things in segments. After she hung up the phone, her relief shone through in her smile.

Poems from the Past

It's worth taking a deeper look at our ambivalence over failed partnerships. This ambivalence can keep us connected to a past that no longer serves us. By hanging on to the relationship through the artifacts that make us remember "when it was good," we derail ourselves from moving forward with what can make us feel connected now.

When I showed up at my client's place, the first thing she said was, "Is it wrong to keep love poems from an ex?" I felt the anguish behind her words.

I said, "Let's start right there."

But then she got overwhelmed by her feelings and didn't want to talk about the poems anymore. That's how powerfully an old relationship can affect us. It lives on within us and feels like too much to look it. But it's never too much. My client's question indicated that she was already feeling bad about these poems, and that alone was reason enough to look at them. Ignoring pain does not make it go away.

I asked her to go get the poetry. She went to her closet and reached under a stack of books and papers and pulled out a notebook. She sat on her couch with the love poems on her lap. Her face looked pinched.

I said, "It looks like they are sucking the life right out of you. Can we let them go?"

She said, "But what if these poems are really good, and I can get them published, and this will let other people have the chance to read something that's great literature?"

As with the divorced woman and her wedding dress, this client justified keeping the poems for the benefit of others. But her voice had the same flatness people have when they don't believe what they are saying. She was hypnotized by her attachment to her old feelings for this relationship. When we are taken out of the moment by unresolved feelings, we can't see clearly, and we may justify doing something that is hurting us. In her mind, she was trying to hold on to her connection with her ex. Maybe she believed she would feel even more pain if she let him go.

I told her that she could try to publish the poems, but that would mean she would have to focus on them for a while. She would have to work hard on their behalf. Could she do that if they caused her so much pain? I reminded her, "The presence of these poems hurts you so much that you had to keep them hidden away in a closet with a lot of books and papers on top of them."

Her eyes cleared. She understood what was happening. She took a deep breath and put the poems on her coffee table.

She said, "He was very abusive. Whenever I got close to him, he would be mean to me. I thought I could get him to open up. I was thinking if I could publish his poems, then he'd love me. But that's not going to happen."

I opened a recycling bag. I said, "If you'd like."

She picked up the notebook, chucked it into the bag, and smiled.

There's a beauty in people's faces when the spell of an old relationship breaks. They become present. You can feel the whole room relax.

EXERCISE

You're an archaeologist in your own home! You're going on a search for objects that were given to you or owned by people who used to be but are no longer part of your life. Your mission is to dig up the broken crockery of your own ancient history.

It helps to remember where things come from. Sometimes we become unconscious of our associations with objects in our environment. Our past, good and bad, can be displayed all around us, and we glaze over it, not realizing how stuck we are in memories of lost loves. But those people aren't here. How would *they* feel if they knew we were getting rid of these things? It doesn't matter.

The great thing is...it's your home. You get to search for, find, and discard whatever you want. If you don't like something, and the bad memories it calls up hamper your joy today, toss it. If something makes you happy, keep it.

Make sure to look through closets. Closets are hiding places for ancient remnants. Look for an item that is emotionally loaded. You'll know it when you uncover it. Sometimes your breath stops. You'll feel tension in your body. You'll want to rebury this thing. It will feel like a bully intimidating you in your own home.

The antidote is realizing that you don't want to live with these kinds of feelings. No one wants to be in pain, physically or emotionally. Anything that warps us doesn't serve us. Dig it out of the ground. Smooth the earth and ready it for new buildings, a living city. Don't live on the crumbled foundations of the past.

Keep the archaeological dig going through all parts of your home. When you find these disturbers from the past, donate, recycle, or toss them. The sooner they go, the better you'll feel.

Our Hearts Remember

I've worked with many people whose parents or beloved family members have died and left them with inheritance clutter. This can be furniture, books, letters, photographs, papers, clothes, cars, property — anything the relative once owned. I call it clutter because my clients often don't care about the majority of the stuff, but they can't let it go because its connection to the deceased makes them feel like they are letting the person go. The situation makes them feel depressed, tired, and overwhelmed.

When a family member or loved one passes away, we inherit things that remind us of them. Most of the time, the items themselves serve no other purpose. By hanging on to these mementos, we attempt to maintain our connection with the person who died. But in most cases this makes for a weak connection. Nothing fully replaces the deceased person's presence. Our longing remains unmet.

When it comes to inherited items, the feelings of loss and longing are often mixed with resentment for having to keep or care for stuff we don't really want. We may even feel angry that the person who died burdened us with all their crap. This anger hurts because we don't want to feel this way about someone we loved. The mixture of sorrow, loss, resentment, guilt, and anger creates a very difficult emotional knot that often causes people to shut down. Usually nothing gets done. People hang on to the items, not knowing what to do with them and thus keep alive their sadness about their loved one's passing.

I was working with a client in her condo. She used to share the space with her mom, who had passed away a few years ago. The place was jam-packed with stuff. Things were piled on top of things, and there was very little floor space. Half the stuff was her mom's.

I decided to start in the living room. Two bookcases were filled with hundreds of her mom's paperback murder mysteries. My client said that she wanted to keep them. I asked if she read them. First she was silent. Then she said no. She said that she listened to books on tape while commuting on the train to work. She looked at the books and was frustrated and angry. She didn't care for murder mysteries at all, but she couldn't let them go. She said she felt her mom had put her in a very difficult spot.

It's natural when a parent dies to want to preserve their things. Their stuff contains their presence, their attention, their personality. It's as if a person's scent lives on in their things. Though they are gone, it feels like they are still with us. And if those things remain an active part of our lives, it serves us to keep them. But often they aren't, and they clog up our living space. My client didn't read these books, but she missed her mom. Part of her felt that if she let go of the books, she'd be letting go of her mom.

But the reverse is true: when we let go of the things from our parents that don't matter to us, our memories of them are no longer clogged up in their stuff. Our parents become a living presence in our hearts, where they resonate much more strongly.

My client agreed to go through the books with me. About 98 percent of them went into the donation pile. She kept a few. She said it made her feel good to see them on the shelf; it was as if her mom were winking at her.

Our homes are not museums, or mausoleums, for loved ones who have passed. We don't cherish the people in our lives by hanging on to them through things we don't care for. We cherish them by living an unencumbered life and being free in our hearts to remember who they were to us.

We can honor our loved ones in ways that don't interrupt our life. We can keep just enough to remind us of the place where our memories and our loved one's presence actually reside: in our hearts. In themselves, things remember nothing. But our hearts can conjure the presence of those we love anytime, and in ways that are fresh and alive.

When a Blessing Becomes a Curse

My client's mom had passed away five years ago, and he had filled one room in his home with everything he'd inherited from her. The room was stuffed full of stacked boxes, and he hated being in it. He thought about doing something with his inheritance every day, but he couldn't take action. The stuff was too emotionally loaded, and he shut down. If his kitchen trash can had gotten knocked over, he would know to immediately clean everything up. But the emotional hold of clutter goes beyond the intellect and frustrates us.

When I asked my client what he wanted to do with the room, he told me he wanted it to be a guest bedroom. I quietly suggested we start to make that happen by going through the contents of the first box within reach. The grip of clutter is loud and chaotic, so it helps to be gentle and matter-of-fact and to keep the goals simple.

With a recycling bag at my side, I picked up a handful of papers from a box and set them on the empty top of a dresser. My client picked up the first paper, which was a letter to his mom from one of her friends. He read it. He started to get lost in it. I asked him what it was. He sighed.

He looked around at the boxes in the room and said, "It's almost a curse I inherited this stuff."

I told him I'd worked with a lot of clients who felt the same way. Their inheritance doesn't feel like a curse because they don't like their parents; it feels like one because they do. They are overwhelmed with sorrow over their parents' deaths, and they don't have the capacity to make decisions about stuff they don't really care about.

At the same time, their resentment gets mixed in with the love because their parents left them in this awful situation. "I miss them, and they dumped all this crap on me!"

My clients worry. If they get rid of their parents' things, are they dishonoring them or their memory? An intuitive part of them knows this isn't true, but this part can be hard to access. It's hard to discern a healthy approach when everything feels so painful. It helps to accept that this is what's happening to you, and it sucks. That recognition helps the healing start to happen.

My client got some peace of mind from this perspective. He wanted to turn this room into a guest bedroom, and there was no reason his inheritance should keep him from creating one. We went back to clutter busting, and he was able to look at each of his mother's possessions and let go of most of her things. We worked for about three hours and filled four big donation bags with his mom's old stuff. This made him very happy.

Similarly, I had a client who had inherited a five-hundred-piece china set from her great-aunt twenty years earlier. However, my client had never used the china, and she hated the set. For twenty years she had lived with the pain and inconvenience of having the set in her home. Why? Because her mom guilt-tripped her into keeping the dishes.

It isn't only our own feelings for the deceased we need to deal with when trying to sort through an inheritance. Other family members can have strong feelings about certain heirlooms. Family pressure to keep things we don't want only further clutters our memories of the person we loved. But there is a way through this.

I asked my client to tell me what she had liked about her great-aunt. She told me that she loved the memory of her great-aunt swimming every day, up into her eighties. This had inspired my client's own daily swim. She said she wanted to keep that memory because it made her feel good, but that she could lose the china. When she told me she had decided to donate the entire set to a church rummage sale, she sounded relieved.

When we guilt-trip others we are trying to control someone's actions because we are afraid of being hurt. My client's mother was probably motivated by the same fear as my client — that if they let the china go, they'd be "letting go" of their beloved aunt. In any case, whatever the mother's agenda was, it didn't serve my client, whose precious feeling of connection to both her great-aunt and her mother was suffering.

When we become aware of the presence of guilt, we have an opportunity to stop and reconsider. What action would increase love and connection right now? If we can refrain from shutting down because of our sadness and fear of loss, we can stay open and see what our hearts tell us to do.

The best gift we can give our loved ones after we die is not to leave them with our piles of clutter. We can do something about this by going through our things now so that they don't become a tangled mess by the time we're gone. And we get the added benefit of a clutter bust while we're still alive!

• How tangled are your finances? I once clutter busted for a woman whose father had died five years earlier, and the family was still unsure about where half of his money was. The private investigators they'd hired were discovering money hidden away in accounts in other countries. Once you die, you'll want your loved ones to find your money. You certainly won't need it anymore. Go through your financial papers and get rid of any paperwork that doesn't represent your current financial situation, such as closed credit card and bank accounts. Then arrange your finances in a way that would make sense to a stranger.

• Do you have clothing you no longer wear? Donate it now. I've helped clients for whom over half their inheritance was clothes their deceased relatives no longer wore, some of which the Smithsonian would probably have been interested in.

- Let go of old technology you no longer use. I once clutter busted a client whose dad had left him with more than two hundred cameras, most of them broken.
- Keep clutter busting all the rooms in your home, thinking of what message you want to leave the people closest to you.

Hopefully you'll stick around for a long time. But now when you do kick the bucket, people won't be wishing you'd taken the time to clutter bust first. Plus, you'll be a lot happier with the time you have left!

Relationships with the Dead Are Still Alive

The following passage is taken from a beautiful email I got from one of my clients, whose father had died, about the freedom she felt after clutter busting:

For more than thirty-five years I've had an unused beach towel. My father gave it to me when I was little. It has managed to stay with me through many moves across the country and back. When I decided to clutter bust the linen closet this week, I felt extreme resistance. I would see the neatly folded towel every time I opened the door.

It finally "spoke" to me, repeating what its message has always been, though I didn't realize it. "Your father died when you were little, and this is all you have left of him. This is the only thing you still have that he gave you."

This message to myself was bringing me down. I also realized it was false. My father gave me important values — to treat people and animals kindly and to be generous. The towel was getting in the way of my realizing that the gifts he had given me were intangible, inside me, and how I strive to live my life every day.

It was with great relief that I put the towel in a bag of clean blankets for a local animal shelter. I felt happy that it would be providing a little comfort, however brief, to a cold puppy. An obstacle has been removed. I feel emotionally lighter. And closer to my father.

At a clutter-busting workshop, one of the participants brought in a photo album, a gift from her sister, who had passed away five years earlier. She was feeling a lot of conflict about what to do with the album. She said it meant a lot to her that her sister had made it, emphasizing that the photo album had been made with love.

Then she surprised herself by saying that she didn't like the album itself and that she wished it wasn't in her house. She agonized over the situation. She wished she could let go of the album, but she was worried that her sister would be hurt, even though she was no longer alive. Then she spoke of a framed photo that her sister had given her of the two of them. It was clear she relished its presence in her home. When she described her feelings about this photo, her words were simple and strong.

I pointed out that the album had become a source of conflict. She didn't like the album, but she felt that tossing it would be like tossing away the love that had inspired the gift. It tore her heart every time she encountered it and cluttered her memories of her sister. But the framed photo of the two of them nurtured her heart and helped her remember her love for her sister.

She thought about it quietly. Then she said that she wished she could feel it was okay to make decisions about the things in her home. She wished she had the authority, but in this case, she had given it away in order to appease her sister.

I told her that she did have the authority. We all have the courage and the insight to say no to the things that we don't want in our homes. The love behind the sister's gift would remain, no matter what happened to the album. We can't give up control of our lives in the hopes of managing how others will feel, even those who have died. Our loved ones live on in our hearts, and that's where this struggle takes place. Our responsibility is to take care of ourselves. When we take care of our needs this way, we open our hearts. When we act out of fear in order to make someone happy, we end up harming our connection. Caring for and experiencing this connection, even with the deceased, within our hearts is the only thing that makes us happy in our relationships.

She reflected on this a moment, took the photos out of the album, and set the album aside in a donate pile.

EXERCISE

Do you have lots of mementos? Are they items you inherited or that embody the memory or legacy of a friend or family member who has passed on? Do you keep stuff to remember people who are still alive but whom you're no longer in touch with?

Go through your home and collect all these items and place them in one room. The objects can be books, clothing, kitchenware, toys, musical instruments, and photos. Sit with them. Talk with each object as if you were talking with the person who died or with whom you are no longer in touch. Describe what the object reminds you of and what it represents. Tell it whatever you'd like. Listen to what each object has to say. Was it important to the person you got it from? This is an opportunity to enjoy the connection you had with your loved one again. You want the connection to move from the things and into your heart. Your heart has unlimited storage capacity. It's your true treasure chest.

When you are done, decide what objects you can let go of, and remove them. If you still enjoy and use certain items, keep them and put them in places where you can interact with and see them.

Trying to Fix the Broken Past

Naturally, inheritance clutter can encumber our memories of people we loved and felt close to. But what happens when our relationships with deceased relatives or friends were themselves painful? Sometimes, our unmet desire to heal these relationships can lead us to hold on to artifacts that we don't even realize are in themselves debilitating.

I was working with a client in his bedroom. He had a cabinet at the end of his bed. I was suspicious of it because when he walked past it, he seemed woozy, almost as if he was momentarily drunk.

I asked him about the history of the cabinet, and he looked fearful. I could feel his inner panic. He said it was his father's liquor cabinet. His dad was an alcoholic who drank himself to death. My client was also an alcoholic but had been sober for twenty years. He was also fifty-nine, the same age as his dad when he died from alcoholism.

I said, "The foot of the bed is your place of stability. For you it's your dad's liquor cabinet, the thing that destroyed him and your family and that almost destroyed you. Can we stop the legacy and toss it out?"

My client agreed. The color returned to his face, and

he emanated strength. We carried the cabinet out to the curb.

Kind Preparation

Clients who have inherited clutter often describe the various difficulties and the pain they experienced with a relative before that person died. They had some type of relationship clutter with that person when they were alive, and now they have inherited a bunch of the deceased relative's stuff. Sometimes, the inheritance clutter itself seems like the deceased person's way of expressing, perhaps unconsciously, the unresolved emotions in the relationship. Whatever the case, my clients often reveal that the turbulence that existed in the relationship still remains. In these situations, we are often hit by a double whammy: we want to protect ourselves from unresolved anger and hurt, but the distance we create from these feelings, though it may make us feel safe and give us a sense of power, only further clutters our connection with our hearts. We may feel devastated, and our anxious efforts to avoid this pain only breed more chaos and make us less capable of finding resolution and peace.

Do you own anything that once belonged to a deceased parent or relative and makes you feel weak? It can be either something you inherited or a gift you were given. The point is that it's in your home and adversely affecting you. Do you have unresolved issues with that person? If so, it's worth removing those things and, at the same time, letting go of any lingering animosity and hurt. We don't lose anything, and we regain the connection within ourselves and our peace of mind. It can be hard to argue with or say no to a parent. But it's always beneficial to say yes to yourself. When you take care of your connection with your heart, you keep yourself alive and aware, available to be in relationship with others.

Coming Back to the Present

When past relationships negatively affect our lives, we lose our flow, bringing things to a halt. We feel that we need to honor the past in some way, that it's sacred. But when doing so takes us out of this present moment, it spoils our life. The truth is, we can't live in two moments at the same time.

I was sitting on the floor with my client, three big containers of photos sitting next to us. The majority of the photos were still in their sleeves from when she had gotten them back from the lab. There was a small group of other photos in frames or lying loosely between the packages.

When we began going through the photos, she immediately shut down. She said, "I don't want to do this. Why do I have to do this? It's a big waste of my time." Her voice was a high whine. She sounded depressed. She added, "I just really hate myself these days. I can't think of one good thing in my life. I hate living like this." She started to weep.

I said, "That's okay. You're stuck. You're not Superwoman. No one is."

Just because we can be decisive about some things doesn't mean we can be fully capable in every moment.

We all get overwhelmed. It helps to recognize when we are feeling diminished and need additional kindness. We can then be present with the situation as it is and respond with sensitivity.

I said, "There are a lot of emotions in photos. Sometimes they remind us of things that we don't want to remember or feel. But if we leave them here, they'll still continue to make you feel this uneasiness, and over a period of time that takes a heavy toll. So, let's look through the photos and find the ones that don't make you feel good anymore."

I handed her a pack of photos to look through. They were pictures from when she was a little girl and showed her family members getting drunk at a party. She told me that she comes from a family of alcoholics, adding that her dad was a "dead man walking." It felt like the photos were sucking the life out of her. She said, "I don't know what to do with these." She was overwhelmed with feelings.

I told her that when she was a little girl, her family was supposed to take care of her. When they couldn't, she began to live in fear. It was like living on a fault line with constant earthquakes. Her life was at stake. This woman was now grown-up, independent, and capable, but the fear was still there. That's why it was hard for her to let the pictures go. She didn't feel safe, even though she was. I said, "You can take care of yourself. These people that weren't capable of taking care of you are no longer alive. But you're alive. You can say no to things that hurt you and remove them from your life."

She looked through these photos and tossed them out.

Then she looked through another stack of pictures from when she became an adult. She tossed the pictures that didn't mean anything to her or that made her sad. We ended up going through all the photos. She found some that made her happy now and set those aside. The heavy-laden fear was gone. My client felt stronger and quieter.

When we become emotionally worn down and overwhelmed by trying to live with the side effects of old relationships, it becomes difficult to function. We are in pain and want to do something about it, but we don't feel capable. We may even give up trying. When we're this depleted, we often can't see what's happening. We may even resent and become angry with the people who try to help us; even offers of help can seem like a threat.

The first step is to recognize that feeling overwhelmed pulls us away from the present. Rather than focusing on trying to resolve the past, try focusing on creating a supportive environment right now by removing any items that undermine your peace of mind. Maybe you can't change or fix the past, but you can take charge of the way you live now. When we loosen our grip on the past, we begin to get our lives back.

Invasion of the Body Snatchers

I was asking my client about the things she kept in her office space. Things were going along well when suddenly a critical voice piped up, and she started to comment harshly on her ability to get things done. Her voice had changed. It had a shrill tone, and she spoke much more quickly. It sounded as if someone inside her was punching away. I distracted her by getting back to the things in the room.

·She was responding well until a few minutes later, when that same critical voice showed up. It sounded like she was imitating someone, but she didn't realize she was doing it. The voice said, "God, I can't believe how much I waste my time. Something must be wrong with me. I don't know why I can't just take care of these things. I feel like I'm wrecking everything."

I told her she was being hard on herself and that it was getting in the way of taking care of what was in front of her. I commented on how it looked like she was punching herself with her words, how she winced from their impact. My client then snapped out of the trance, and her breathing returned to normal. Her clarity came back. She didn't say anything for a few seconds as a realization kicked in.

As we continued to go through her things, she started talking about her mother. She described how her mom had been critical of her while she was growing up. She imitated her mother for me, and her imitation sounded exactly like her critical voice.

I said, "That was your mom. You were channeling her. Or the way she programmed you to get things done when you were little. It sounded like a recording that was being played back. You faded out, and she came in and spoke to you."

We all have aspects of our parents in us. Our parents taught us how to behave in the world, and they judged us by their standards. But some of the things they taught us turned out to be things we can't use. Sometimes these attitudes are so ingrained in us we don't even question them. I said, "This voice from the past doesn't suit you. It invades your body. It's not your nature. It's clutter."

I sensed that she recognized her mother in herself. It was a sobering experience. Sometimes we can be so attached to a relationship from the past that we don't even recognize the time travel. My client was seeing herself as separate from this maternal echo for the first time. Even though the critical mom voice might (and probably would) crop up again, her awareness had freed her from its negative influence.

Clutter Busting a Past Self

As we grow older, we leave our childhood selves behind. But even as adults, we keep changing and leaving behind our old ways of doing things. Sometimes we feel an attachment to old versions of ourselves and we try to drag them along with us. But these old ways no longer fit our current lives. They end up getting in the way and making things more difficult. But we don't want to let go of them because we remember how they used to protect us or make us happy.

At a clutter-busting talk, a woman in the audience described her own particular clutter predicament. She said that she had a pillow in her trunk that she couldn't throw out. She said it was too dirty to donate and that it couldn't be recycled. The woman couldn't get herself to let it go because she was worried about adding to the landfill. Meanwhile, whenever she opened the trunk of her car, she felt great discomfort. This put her in a constant agitated state.

She said she used to live in a Zen center, and they either recycled or donated everything that was no longer of use to them. She no longer lived there and wanted to continue to hold up the same ideal.

I told her that this way of living served her in the Zen center because they carefully controlled everything that came into their environment. She was happy living that way. She felt connected. But now that way of living was cutting off her connection with herself. That lifestyle was now clutter in her new living space because it didn't support her.

She understood what was happening and agreed to give the pillow to someone at the talk, who would toss it out. She looked relieved.

How do you know when a previous version of yourself has become clutter? It's usually obvious. You'll feel miserable and wish for a return to an earlier time in your life. Time travel is fun, but it's not as much fun as being in relationship with yourself and others right now. That's the big adventure that awaits.

EXERCISE

Let's go for an exploratory walk in your home. We're looking for things that are "unplugged," that are no longer connected to you. When we love something, we give it juice, just like we plug a toaster into a wall socket when we want to use it. But when something no longer serves us, when we don't use it, it becomes unplugged from us. These things actually lose their luster. They often remain in our homes because we simply don't notice them anymore.

But today, we are looking for what no longer shines. Walk into each room and scan for dull, dusty things. If you go slowly and pay attention to your reactions, you'll know these items when you see them: you get tired, you want to look away, you try to distract yourself with something else, you feel guilty, you put yourself down, you want to cover up or hide this thing, you feel shame, or you try to defend your desire to keep this thing (even though you don't use it). All these reactions are "out of sorts" detectors indicating that your connection with this thing is gone.

It's okay to admit, "This thing no longer does it for me." You wouldn't eat stale, moldy food. You wouldn't wear a shirt that was two sizes too small. You wouldn't drive a car with a flat tire. It's okay to let go of what's not serving you.

Pick up these artifacts as you find them. If they are broken, toss them. If they still function, donate them to a charity. As you do, you'll begin to feel reconnected to yourself.

What does your present self love? Find these objects and display them for hands-on access for your everyday adventures.

Chapter Seven

WHEN A RELATIONSHIP BECOMES CLUTTER

At what point does a relationship itself become clutter? In chapter 4, I described relationships as tangible things. We create a relationship together, and we tend to our connection. Yet despite our best efforts, we may find that a relationship has stopped serving us. Maybe we just don't enjoy it anymore, or maybe it's causing us great emotional pain. The relationship now affects our well-being and other aspects of our lives.

Yet despite recognizing a relationship as clutter, we can't let it go. We are conflicted and ambivalent, and we resist making a change. Our good-faith attempts to fix it seem to fail. But since we are attached to our memories of when it was a positive part of our life, we continue with the hope that the relationship will improve, even though there's no evidence to support this.

No one can tell us when we should give up on a relationship. But when you remain in a relationship that has turned into clutter, it is no different from piling clutter in your living room: it's painful and exhausting. It diminishes your ability to make decisions. It limits your life and hurts your sense of self. You end up living in a limited way. You can even start believing you are a diminished person.

But you're not. You're more than you can imagine.

I want to make clear that we're not talking about evaluating or judging the other person. When we clutter bust a relationship, we take an honest look at how being in a relationship with this person affects us. We ask, "How does being with this person make me feel? Does this relationship serve and nourish me or not?" This chapter is about seeing whether a relationship has become clutter. If it has, then with the same nonjudgmental awareness we bring to clutter busting our things, we let it go.

Unwanted Baggage

I worked with someone who was in pain from the emotional abuse she was receiving from a friend. Her friend had stayed with her for a few months while separated from her husband. She had verbally lashed out at my client a number of times and made my client feel like she was to blame for her own chaotic state. The friend had stayed with her more than a year ago, but my client was still bruised and trying to recover. She had a bag of things that her friend had left at her house. She had tried to return them to her friend, but the friend had sent them back with a verbally abusive handwritten note. My client was left feeling guilty.

It can be hard to tell someone that we are upset about

how they are treating us. We may feel that this will upset *them* and that they will leave the friendship. There is security in things as they are. If the person gets upset and leaves us, we might hurt even worse. This is one reason we choose to remain in emotional pain. But this means we are damaging our connection with ourselves in order to preserve a connection with someone else. Because we're fearful, we are knocked out of our essential relationship with ourselves. And yet, we can't preserve a connection with someone else when we're not present to ourselves. Our connection to ourselves is one half of any relationship.

My client showed me her friend's bag. As she held it, she sulked. She was blaming herself for her friend's reactions. She kept thinking of where she had gone wrong. I told her that she was punishing herself for no reason. She had done nothing wrong. Her friend had been in a fractured state and had manipulated my client to keep from feeling the pain of her life in that moment.

As it turned out, this wasn't the first time something like this had happened. My client described other times when her friend had emotionally abused her. She recognized the guilt she was carrying as clutter and decided it was time to stand up for herself. She came out of her clutter trance and threw the bag of stuff in the trash. There was color in her face again. Her voice grew stronger. She decided to no longer have contact with her former friend.

The kind of protection that is most valuable to us is protecting our first relationship: our connection to ourselves. When we recognize that we are being hurt, rather than pulling inward to try to escape the blows, we learn to *remove the source of the pain*. If someone else's stuff, or presence, is causing us chronic grief and sorrow, it's okay to remove the thorn in our side and let the relationship go. Of course, all relationships go through rough times, and this doesn't mean you need to end them. But sometimes relationships clearly no longer serve the people in them. Below, I explain how to tell the difference between a relationship that is going through a difficult time and one that needs to be let go.

I was working with another client in the guest room of her house. A friend had stayed there two years earlier and had overstayed her welcome. We'll call her friend "the Visitor." The Visitor was supposed to be there a very short time and ended up staying for many months. This had a negative effect on my client's family. They didn't feel at home in their own house while the Visitor was there.

My client was feeling out of sorts about it all. She felt guilty about her family's experience. She was angry with the Visitor for not being a good guest. She was upset that she let someone take advantage of her. Plus, she was bothered by the amount of stuff the Visitor had left behind. Her conflicted feelings had caused her to shut down and not do anything about it for two years. She was feeling bad about shutting down as well.

She thought of the Visitor as her friend. She didn't even consider telling her friend that the stuff she had left at the house had to go. She felt that keeping the stuff was something she just had to endure. But this was just prolonging the conflict, at least in her own heart. Perhaps she knew that returning the Visitor's things would mean ending their relationship, or perhaps she hoped the Visitor would notice and acknowledge the burden my client had accepted. The only thing that actually mattered was that the presence of the Visitor's stuff was hurting her. It was clutter.

To sidestep the clutter of blame, I told her that none of this was her fault. It's what happened. Sometimes circumstances add up, and we are too overwhelmed or exhausted to act. But it's worth noticing when the presence of the stuff in our homes negatively affects us. Seeing this clearly can help inspire us to let it go so we can start to feel good in our homes again.

Without the weight of blame, my client recognized the dynamics of her situation. She started to relax, and she agreed that the solution was to pack up everything and send it back to the Visitor. We went through drawers, closets, and boxes. She was amazed at how much stuff the Visitor had left in her home. The Visitor was like a tree with many, many roots.

We put the Visitor's things in boxes, and we taped the boxes up and addressed them. Then my client sent an email to the Visitor that she was sending back her things. We stood in the guest room and experienced the change. By this point, my client had realized what she was really letting go of: her desire for the friend's approval, which had undermined her own sense of self.

She said, "She's not my friend. I let her take advantage of me because I thought she was a really neat person.

I wanted her to want me as her friend. But I really sold myself short. I'm worth a lot more than this."

Yay! It always delights me to see my clients reclaim themselves!

EXERCISE

In this exercise, you will create a drawing that embodies your relationship with someone you're in conflict with. On a large, blank sheet of paper, write the name of the person on one side. Next to or near their name, make a simple drawing that represents them. It doesn't have to look like them. It could be a stick figure, a tree, or an abstract shape — whatever comes to mind. You're looking to capture your essential perception of them.

Next to this drawing, draw an image of yourself in relation to this person. How does this person affect you? Do you shine? Are you deflated? Are you richer? Do you shrink? Is one of you more powerful? Remember, they'll never see this drawing, so you can be as wild and detailed as you'd like. Add and embellish until the drawing captures the essence of your feelings. We can often be more expressive when we don't use words.

Take a look at what you drew. Now imagine

your drawing hanging in a gallery. Step back and look at it objectively. What feelings does it bring up? How would you describe the drawing to a stranger? What's obvious about it? What type of relationship do you see? How would you feel if this picture were hanging in your home?

We can get so used to being in a relationship that we don't notice the effect it has on us, good or bad. When we clutter bust, we are looking to see whether or not something is serving us, and by making a drawing of our relationships, we are uncovering our feelings about the people in our lives.

Hiding behind the Desk

In the middle of my client's living room was a big, bulky desk covered with papers, books, junk mail, CDs, and pet supplies. The desk intimidated her. She couldn't think clearly enough to make a decision about its fate. When I asked her if she used it, she said she didn't. Then I asked where she got it. She whispered that her mother had given it to her. She said she couldn't give it away because her mother would get angry with her. She visibly shrank when she spoke these words.

I sensed that her mother was living in her house as the desk. I asked her if she wanted to live with her mother's presence, since it seemed to have the effect of making her shut down and lose her stability.

My client explained that she was estranged from her mother. A while back, her mom had stolen some of her credit cards and purchased thousands of dollars' worth of things. My client didn't press charges or get angry with her mom. She simply canceled the card. But she didn't ask her mother, who lived a few states away, to pay her back. They rarely talked, and when they did, her mother would emotionally abuse her. Her relationship with her mother was causing her great emotional disturbance. But she didn't want to let it go.

My client had chosen to live with the terror and pain of her mom's abusive behavior rather than standing up to her mother and risking being abandoned by her. But though she was trying to preserve the relationship, her experience with the desk showed this wasn't working. The desk embodied all her conflicted emotions and pain and diminished her ability to function in her daily life. Maintaining her relationship with her mother came at a direct personal cost to her relationship with herself. Of course, since her connection with herself was lost, she was not preserving her relationship with her mother in any real way. The desk had to go.

I said, "Your mom stole money from you. She committed a felony. She beats you up emotionally when you talk. You live in fear of what she might do next. Yet you say you want to keep this altar to her in your living room. You try to cover it up with these things you put on the desk. But it's still hurting you."

My client worried about how painful it would be to tell her mom no about anything, including the desk. But she was already living in pain and constant fear because of her mother. I told her she was now an adult who was in charge of her life, not a little girl who still needed to be taken care of. Her life was now in her hands, not her mom's. She could responsibly and powerfully say no to things that were hurting her.

My client sat quietly, and then she nodded. She called her mom and told her she was letting go of the desk. When her mom launched into her, my client winced, but then she cut her off and said, "Mom, you stole money from me. I can't trust you! It makes me so angry that you did that!" Her mom got defensive. My client cut her off again, saying, "I don't want to hear your excuses. I'm mad at you. I'm sorry you don't want to hear that, but it's what I'm feeling. And I'm getting rid of the desk. I've got to go." She hung up and looked at me, clear faced and shining.

She said, "God, that felt good."

We got rid of most of the things on the desk. Then we took the desk outside to the curb. When we came back in, she stood in the empty space where the desk had been. My client and her living room both seemed renewed.

My client didn't let go of the relationship. But she clutter busted how she interacted with her mom, exchanging it for a way of communicating that served her. Rather than trying to hide behind the desk for protection, she defended herself in a healthy way by standing up and removing the desk, which was hurting her.

When a relationship is causing us harm, we clutter bust that relationship and create a new one with the person. If the other person refuses to change, then for our own well-being, we may have to let that person go. We may fear hurting them with our actions, but in all likelihood the relationship isn't serving them, either. It's okay to ask, "Does having this person in my life serve and inspire me? Or is their presence in my life hurting me?" Despite what we may think, it doesn't serve anyone to maintain an unhealthy relationship.

Drunk in Our Space

One of my clients was living with his girlfriend. She was an alcoholic and wasn't taking care of herself. She became distant and rarely communicated with him. He kept his feelings about this to himself, and yet he had affairs with other women. He didn't tell his girlfriend about these other relationships, and this caused him a lot of guilt. He said he felt obligated to stay with his girlfriend because they had been together a long time. But he sounded tired when he talked about the situation.

My client had also let his father move in with him. His father was a practicing alcoholic who would drink all day and lapse into a semicomatose state. Sometimes his dad would fly into a drunken rage and break things. This was hard for my client because he himself was an alcoholic who was trying to stay sober. But he was afraid to tell his dad to leave. He said he turned back into a little boy when he was around his dad. He lost his own connection and couldn't stand up for himself.

I said it sounded as if he was disintegrating inside by living this way. My client told me that he'd gotten so disconnected from himself that he'd let a lot of his life turn into clutter. He'd hired me to help him deal with his things, but it was clear that his relationships with his live-in girlfriend and father were the major sources of his clutter.

Life becomes difficult when we get disconnected from ourselves, because we can't think clearly. Without our clarity, we don't notice the details of what's happening. We lose our ability to see whether things are serving us or causing us harm. We get caught up in the swell. It's often at this time that we blame ourselves for our circumstances. Blame usually just makes us feel worse, further weakening and reducing our clarity. The first and best thing we can do is to recognize that we are in great pain and that we don't like it. This acknowledgment allows us to take care of what needs changing in a way that makes a positive difference.

I told my client that it sounded as if he had cut himself off from his heart. His life situation was very painful, so he had decided to live in a way that numbed him. But he could never numb it all away. That's why he still felt sad. He was numb and sad and used to feeling that way.

I said, "It's funny. You're sober, but your life is making you drunk. In the same way you once saw alcohol as clutter, you can now see living with people you don't want to be with as clutter as well." There was recognition in his eyes. I could feel his life flowing back in. Sometimes all we need is a crack of recognition for the light to get in.

When I spoke with my client a few months later, he told me he'd broken up with his girlfriend, who had found a new place to live. And he had told his father to move out. His dad had moved back to his old hometown. My client told me he felt he was getting his strength back. He said that when he was working with me he had been trying to avoid feeling anything because he felt that the pain of it all would destroy him. But it turned out that experiencing his emotions actually made him feel whole.

The clearest signal of whether we are supporting our connection with ourselves or diminishing it comes from asking, "How do I feel in the moment?" This self-awareness and acknowledgment of our feelings is essential, and it can be gained, and practiced, by clutter busting our life.

When we try to maintain a relationship that has turned into clutter, we have to lie to ourselves. It then becomes hard to continue being honest about the other parts of our lives, and we slowly lose connection with ourselves. As with anything consistently present in our lives, we can get used to feeling despair. It becomes normal, and we lose the incentive to help ourselves. That's why I encourage the investigation of clutter busting. We can develop a new habit of seeing whether the people in our lives nourish or deplete us. We can live with basic openness and stay healthy.

Knowing When to Clutter Bust a Relationship

How do you know if you want to leave a relationship because you are afraid of being open and intimate, because you're working through a rough time, or because the relationship itself is unhealthy for you and the other person?

The first thing to recognize is whether fear is keeping you from being open and connected. We're operating from fear when we're excessively angry at or critical of the other person in the relationship, or we remain hidden from them through guilt. Although someone may seem to pose a threat and be your enemy, they may not be. They may be willing to drop their defenses if you will only drop yours. Only by clutter busting yourself will you truly find out.

You drive me
- nuts, but
then I did
get in your car.

But if being open and honest with the other person doesn't resolve the situation, and the relationship still consistently causes you pain and suffering, then you need to find a compassionate way to express your decision to take care of yourself first. When we are compassionate with ourselves, our goal is to create a healthy life, not to blame or judge the other. We're learning how to include ourselves in our relationships. When we show we are not a threat to the other person, they might be encouraged to change and accept the terms of a new relationship with us.

Of course, they may not. And we often resist taking that chance. If the other person doesn't change, we strengthen our resolve by recognizing how damaging and draining the relationship is. Your best resource is to watch this clutter at work. See how it dominates your thoughts. Notice how it closes off your heart. Notice how the relationship hurts other areas of your life. Do you want to continue experiencing these harsh side effects, or do you want to let them go?

When a cluttered situation overwhelms us, we can give up and hope the situation will resolve itself on its own. But that strategy usually creates more clutter, and we retreat within ourselves. It's kind of like leaving a car wreck on the freeway. It's bound to cause more collisions.

I encourage you to remove the wreckage piece by piece and see what's left in the end. Clutter busting our personal space can provide the clarity and peace of mind we need to make a decision. The process works in reverse too: as we become healthy and open in one area of our life, our decision making and clarity in all areas start to improve.

EXERCISE

Do you own any objects that remind you of a past painful relationship? Let's take a tour through your home with an eye for anything that reminds you of an emotionally painful connection with someone from your past.

You might find a jacket from an old lover that brings up bad memories. Perhaps you come across a book given to you by a negative friend who is no longer a part of your life. Maybe there's a piece of furniture that you tend to avoid because it reminds you of a hurtful relationship. I had a client who realized that she kept having a bad night's sleep because she was sleeping in the bed she and her ex had bought together and slept in for fifteen years. She let the bed go.

Because these negative things are often mixed with some positive feelings, they are still in your home. When you come across one of these loaded items, you might find yourself remembering the good experiences you had with the person. But take a step back within yourself and notice the part of you that is trying to forget about the pain. It's a strain to live with emotional hurt. It seeps into the deepest recesses of our hearts. We can't be at peace with something that hurts us.

Today is a good day to remove these things that are hurting you. The quicker you get them out of your house, the sooner you'll feel like yourself again.

The Fear of Open Space

You may discover that resistance to letting go of a cluttered relationship is fear of being alone, which is often the source of clutter. As the clutter begins to go, my clients sometimes feel uncomfortable with their newly unencumbered space. They are no longer buffered from the difficult emotions they don't want to feel, and they find themselves longing for distractions. Rather than experiencing those feelings, it can feel easier to stop letting go and merge with their stuff again.

Being alone can seem worse than living with the pain of a corrosive relationship. But that's a mirage. It's conjecture, not an actual reflection of experience. It's just something the mind throws up as an objection, and that's normal. We have a natural resistance to change, which can be uncomfortable. But wait — so are our painful relationships! Yet there's a tangible difference. We know a negative relationship is damaging; we see the heavy toll it takes on all parts of our lives. The pain of a cluttered relationship lasts as long as we stay in the relationship as it is.

In contrast, change can cause fear, sadness, and discomfort, but the majority of the pain is in the healing. The pieces of our heart are being sewn back together, and the hurt from this is temporary. Soon we will be feeling free — and fantastic.

Chapter Eight

CLUTTER BUSTING TOGETHER

As we recognize the ways that clutter disrupts and intrudes into our relationships, we can start fresh. We can approach our lives in a healthy way. We can befriend ourselves and each other. We're not in competition. When we become healthier and more joyful, so do others, and there's great benefit in working toward this goal together.

This chapter focuses on how to clutter bust your space with the people sharing that space. It can be tricky work, but now that you've learned so much, you're ready for it.

An Invitation

I was working with a client in the alcove just outside her garage. The area was overstuffed with her kids' artwork and with books, newspapers, boxes, and clothes. It was no wonder she was having a hard time thinking clearly.

My client revealed that she was angry that her husband wasn't more responsive about helping her take care of the community space. But when I asked whether she'd requested his help, she said she hadn't. She felt he should just offer it. I wondered aloud whether she was staying angry in the hopes that her anger would affect him and he would change his ways. That got her attention. Then I pointed out that this wasn't working. She needed to change tactics. Her anger was actually getting in the way of effectively taking care of the situation.

She understood and felt some relief. I called her husband over to the alcove and said to him, "Your wife is feeling overwhelmed by this room. I was wondering if you could help us out?"

He was open to it, and so the three of us began clutter busting as a team. I asked them both about each object in the room. They worked well together. When we were done, the woman said to her husband, "I was angry at you because you wouldn't help organize this area. But you didn't know it because I was keeping it all inside. I wanted you to just know it was bothering me. I got mad when you didn't know that."

He said, "I want to help. You can just ask me next time."

"But you always look so busy," she said. "I always think I'd be bothering you."

He smiled and said, "You wouldn't be."

Clutter busting together has only one rule: it must be an invitation. We can't coerce or force someone to do it. If they say no, then that's a conflict we'll have to deal with. But don't assume a negative answer before you ask sincerely and respectfully. When we step out of our armor and ask for help, a beautiful life awaits us.

Clutter Busting Is Not a Punishment

We can't make someone clutter bust because we think they need to get rid of their stuff. I was hired to work with a young girl whose parents tried to make her clutter bust her room with me. She wasn't interested and sat watching TV in another room with her sister. Her dad said, "If you don't get in the room with the clutter buster, he's going to throw out all your things!" Her mom went and got her daughter and brought her into her room. She sternly told her daughter that she had to work with me. The little girl didn't want to do it. She lay facedown on her bed and wouldn't look up.

I knew the parents were nice people. But they were trying to control their daughter, and this clutter had found its way into their relationship. I've seen this many times with parents and children. But there's no openness in control. We need encouragement and kindness to thrive, and without this compassion, we shut down. As you know by now, clutter busting is about much more than just "cleaning up." It's about enhancing our connection to ourselves and others in the present moment. The girl responded to this well-meaning but misguided attempt to control her by completely shutting down. This was her way of wresting control of the situation. I wanted to bring some openness back, on both sides.

I asked the girl how old she was, and she told me she was six. I told her that my girlfriend's son was nine and that

I had helped him clutter bust. I said that he liked giving stuff away that he didn't play with anymore because it went to kids who didn't have toys. Now those kids had more toys to play with.

The little girl turned around, sat up, and smiled at me. I said, "We're just gonna take a look at some of your things and see which ones you like playing with and which ones you don't." I kept it light. I find that the light touch works with adults as well as kids. Everyone wants to be treated kindly. No one likes to be told what to do.

I started going through her toy box. I picked up one toy at a time and asked, "Do you still like playing with this, or can we give it to some other kids?" She said yes or no to each one. There was no hemming or hawing. She knew. "I like that one." "No, you can put that in the other pile." It went pretty quickly. Her mother sat silently throughout. She seemed fascinated that a softer approach worked so well to change her daughter's attitude.

When we were done, the girl seemed happy. She didn't feel like she had lost anything or had it taken from her. She still had the toys that she liked to play with. When we clutter bust together, we are seeking to find and appreciate what we enjoy. We do this by respecting, accepting, and celebrating one another's choices.

Kind Encouragement

Kind encouragement is the most effective and lasting way to help others make positive changes. People used to believe that the best way to motivate others was through intimidation and force. But if we feel someone is holding on to clutter, our criticism and blame only cause more pain; the person will either defend themselves or shut down, but they won't be inspired to make healthy change. Or, if they give in to our pressure and get rid of whatever we think they should, they may resent us. The object may be gone, but now our relationship is cluttered.

If you want to start, I'll be your beginning.

I worked with a client who shared a living space with her daughter. The mother and I were working together well. She was tossing lots of papers that were no longer part of her life. Then her daughter came into the room and began making critical comments about her mother. The daughter compared her mother to the people profiled on a TV show called *Hoarders*, which the daughter said was about people who obsessively collect things they don't use. My client looked dejected and began to slow down her pace. Her daughter said that her mom's clutter situation was out of control and that she should know better. The mother didn't defend herself.

I don't care for the word *hoarder*. It's an uncompassionate way to describe someone who is stuck in a more-than-average amount of clutter. Being called a *hoarder* doesn't inspire a person to let go of their clutter, which was immediately obvious with my client. But also the term is often used as a self-protective defense, as if the person were thinking, "I'm not like those *hoarders*, so I must not have a clutter problem." In my experience, everyone has a clutter problem. And when I come to work in a person's home, whether they have a lot of clutter or a little, I assume that their clutter situation is hurting them. Only with kindness will they find relief.

I said to the daughter, "You're hurting your mom with your words." The daughter said, "No, I'm not. She needs to hear this."

I told the daughter that condemning her mother wasn't working. When she was critical, her mom lost inspiration and gave up. The daughter was clearly in the habit of talking to her mom this way, but she needed to know that it didn't actually help. Her mom and I had been working well together until her daughter offered her criticisms. At that point, the mother retreated inward and shut down. I said that if the daughter used kind encouragement instead, I suspected her mother would rise to the occasion.

The daughter grew quiet and considered what I said.

Her behavior toward her mom was clutter. It wasn't serving their relationship. It was causing pain and getting in the way of effective action. The daughter looked at her mom with tenderness. She said, "Mom, you're doing really great. You've let go of a lot this morning." The mother beamed. It was like the sun had risen in her heart. She said, "Thank you."

I'm never bored seeing how people come to life with encouragement. It's as if our hearts ignite and become the rocket fuel for our lives.

Helping Someone Clutter Bust

Let's start by discussing one person helping someone else clutter bust their things, and then we will turn to two people clutter busting shared items together. It doesn't matter what your relationship is — whether you're family members, friends, coworkers, or partners — or whether you share the living space being clutter busted. You just need to start with awareness and clarity. Both people must be open to the process and their roles. The person facilitating the clutter bust agrees to be open and encouraging, maintaining a safe place in which the other person can consider each object and ask whether to let go of it or keep it.

For the clutter buster, it's your job to keep the process gentle. The other person may at times feel exposed, fragile, and confused, so try to maintain an environment of openness and nonjudgmental awareness.

It's good to keep the questions simple. Pick up one item at a time and ask, "Do you still enjoy this, or can we let it go?" You want to help the other person decide *for themselves* with a yes or no. You can vary the questions, depending on the item or the context: "Would you buy this in a store if you were out shopping today?" "Do you use this, or can we donate it?"

If the person is having difficulty deciding yes or no, chances are the item is clutter for them. In this case, recognize that they are feeling some emotional attachment and be gentle with them. When a person is stuck, an emotional storm is going on within them. Any force, harshness, or criticism adds to the intensity of the storm and distracts them from their purpose. The person being clutter busted shifts their attention to the criticism and away from the task at hand.

Be delicate and practice observing what you see, rather than trying to give advice. It can help to describe the person's manner, such as by saying, "You look like you are in pain when you're holding that. You look very uncomfortable as you are thinking about this thing. Your shoulders are hunched up. Your breathing is tight. Your voice is low. It looks like the lights got turned off inside you." Help the other person see the effect this thing has on them. They may not be aware of this effect, and yet this realization can be all the help they need to see that something is no longer serving them.

Sometimes, the clutter buster feels that something is clutter and the person they are helping doesn't see it. You may feel frustrated by this, but keep this frustration to yourself. I've heard a frustrated helper say to someone,

"Why are you keeping that? You don't need that." This doesn't help the other person, since they feel your frustration, and it adds to their feeling of stuckness. Perhaps the attachment runs deep and is not easily seen or let go of. They need the support of your openness to help them get clarity. Instead of voicing frustrations when they arise, try being silent. This helps the person quiet their own mind and untangle their confusion.

Throughout, be quietly encouraging, saying, "You're doing a really good job." After they get rid of something, say something like, "That was great." Look for ways to show the person how to be nicer to themselves.

It's best for you to honor the person's choices. You may not agree with their decisions. They may want to get rid of something you think they should keep. But that's your opinion about their stuff. We can't know what's best for another person, but that doesn't stop us from trying! I've seen people tell the person they are helping, "Oh, my God, you should keep that; it's great." Or, "You can't get rid of that. It cost too much money." Or, "Why would you want to get rid of something that looks so great on you?" A part of you may be screaming inside to give your opinion. But don't second-guess the person's choices or intuition. Your only role is to help them make decisions for themselves so they can become self-reliant.

Another essential job is for you to guide the clutter bustee to a firm yes or no answer. Don't let them start a "maybe" or an "I'm not sure" pile. Indecision, hesitation, and uncertainty are clutter red flags. They signal that the person still has some attachment to the item. You want to gently help them let go of the habit of automatically hanging on to everything that makes them feel this way. In a way, all the clutter in our homes is one big maybe pile.

Point out how indecision shows up in their physiology: Do they hold their head in their hands, or a hand to their throat? Do their eyes glaze over? Do they look pale? Usually there's a sudden shift, and then they look like they're not feeling well.

I sometimes ask a client, "Do you like the shirt you are wearing? Do you like your shoes?" Chances are they do, since they are wearing them. They'll emphatically say, "Yes!" Point out that when we like something, we say yes easily. If we have to use a lot of words, and defend the thing, chances are it's no longer a part of our life.

As the person makes decisions, take the item and put it in the appropriate place. If it's trash, put it in a trash bag right then and there. If it's going to be donated, put it in a container for charity, and afterward get on the phone and schedule a pickup, or drive the things over to a donation center. If the object is being kept, have the person put it away where they will enjoy it. Once decisions are made, follow through immediately. This provides a feeling of calm, steady progress in what's otherwise a stressful situation.

If you are the person being clutter busted, your job is to be open with each thing presented to you. Everything else you own disappears from your awareness. There's just this one thing. With the assistance of the clutter buster, you are looking at whether or not you love this thing. You are looking with curiosity. "Hm, I wonder, does this thing support me or not?" Answer with a yes or no.

You may feel a strong, overwhelming emotion come up about a certain item. But you're not alone. Take a breath. Take in the support of the person helping you. When they ask, "Is this serving you, or can you let it go?" imagine that it's your voice strongly and calmly asking this question.

The other person is there to help you understand your own emotions and avoid being overwhelmed. Let them be your temporary life raft.

If the clutter-busting session becomes tense, or either of you is getting tired, take a break. Go for a walk, eat something, or get a drink of water. Or just relax and take it easy. There's no deadline. You can set up an appointment to clutter bust tomorrow or later in the week. It doesn't have to be done in one day. You don't want the process of clutter busting to become clutter. You're looking for relief.

The best thing about clutter busting together is that it provides an opportunity for openness to occur in the relationship. All relationships benefit from a safe closeness. We're at our best when we are open, aware, and unguarded. This openness puts both people in connection with themselves, and they become a pleasure to be with.

A woman I know had decided to start living with her boyfriend. He was moving into her place, and she was worried that he would bring all his stuff and she would get overwhelmed. She described him as a pack rat.

She had read my first book, and she told her boyfriend that she had clutter busted some of her stuff to make space for him. She offered to help him do some clutter busting of his stuff before the move. He agreed but said he'd go through just one box of memorabilia with her.

As they went through the items, he would pull something out of the box and say, "Oh, my God, this means so much to me. This was from when I _____." She let him talk, listening gently and kindly as he reminisced and described his feelings. She didn't say, "But you're not using that anymore," or, "Why do you want to keep that?" When he was done talking about each item, she knew to softly ask, "Do you still want this, or can we let it go?" She let him choose without commenting or trying to influence him. She said he was surprised to find himself letting go of most of the things in the box. He felt so good afterward that he decided to go through another box with her. They continued to clutter bust until the move-in date.

I like this story for several reasons. They took their time. There was no harshness or pressure. She considered and acknowledged her boyfriend's feelings. Sometimes we need a few minutes with an item to experience our feelings about it, but once we do, we can move on.

I also enjoyed hearing about the kindness and trust they showed each other. The girlfriend was scared initially about all her boyfriend's things coming into her home, but she didn't let her fears take control and distort their connection. She didn't insist up front that they clutter bust *all* his things. Then, in the moment, she stayed open and present for him so he could be open and present for himself. For his part, the boyfriend was able to open up to letting go, and he trusted his girlfriend to guide him. This simple, mutual trust was wonderful preparation for their life together.

Clutter Busting Together

I was working with a couple in their bedroom. They were in a pretty good mood until they stood by the bed. The man looked happy. But the woman had her arms tightly crossed and was brooding.

I said to them, "Do you both like this bed?" At the same moment, he said, "Yes," and she said, "No!" They looked at each other in surprise. He said to her, "I thought you liked it." She said with tremendous feeling, "I've never liked the frame." I said, "How long have you been sleeping on this bed?" "Eight years," she replied. "I've always hated it." "How come you didn't say anything?" he said to her. "Well," she said, "you really liked it, so I didn't want to say anything."

I said, "It's important to have a bed that you both love. Can we let the bed frame go?"

They both agreed. We dismantled the frame and took it outside. He called a charity group to come and pick it up. Then they went online and looked at bed frames. They picked and ordered one they both loved.

This couple barely needed my help. They were able to play both clutter-busting roles at once: they focused on their own emotional reactions while providing a safe environment for the other to do the same. That's the goal of clutter busting together. It's the job of each clutter buster to see and take care of their own things — and reactions — and to respect the things and feelings belonging to the other person.

Okay, that's the goal. But it's not always so easy. People

can develop a lot of automatic reactions to one another, and these reactions are clutter in the relationship. Exposing these reactions in a nonjudgmental way creates a flow between people, increasing connection and compassion. When people work together, they can agree to recognize their own tense and reactive feelings. But what if the battle of wanting to keep something versus wanting to get rid of it is occurring because of cluttered mechanics in the relationship?

It helps to slow things down and talk honestly with the other person about your feelings. It's better to agree to disagree about an object than to try to convince the other they are wrong. No object is important enough to distort and spoil your relationship. By working together in this way, you are making your relationship a priority over everything else. If you need perspective, you can even ask each other, "Is this relationship important to us, or do we want to let it go?" Usually the answer is a triumphant, "Yes, it's important!" With this awareness of what really matters, you can continue with your clutter bust.

Creating a Safe Haven for Honesty

Sometimes one member of a couple will silently endure a shared item that they dislike. They keep the peace by letting it be. But meanwhile the presence of this thing agitates them daily. This negatively affects the overall health of the partnership, which they are trying to maintain by their silence. In contrast, being matter-of-fact and open about your feelings brings back the flow that is the lifeblood of a relationship.

I was working with a couple in their home. The woman was letting go of a lot of things, but the man was resistant. He didn't think that the clutter busting was necessary. They began to argue, and things got heated.

When I asked the man what was bothering him, he began to complain about his parents. They had died, and he was left with a house full of their stuff. He said it was an agonizing experience to have to wade through it and figure out what to keep and what to throw out. He was feeling very emotional. His wife started to argue with him, saying this was reason enough for them to clutter bust, so their kids didn't have to deal with the same situation. He got angry that she was telling him what to do.

I told them they were both feeling emotional and that the clutter was affecting them. It's not easy being vulnerable with another person. It can be hard enough to admit to *ourselves* when we feel vulnerable. We get scared when we feel like we can be hurt. We can also be reminded of things that have hurt us in the past. As we go through our stuff, it shakes up feelings we may have long avoided, and that can make us uncomfortable. To protect ourselves from these feelings, we may argue with the person we are clutter busting with. But this is a distraction from the real issue, and it creates and fuels the tension and irritability we are feeling. It helps to recognize when this happens. When we can have this awareness, we ease off and express tenderness for each other. Compassion creates a safe haven for honesty.

When I told them this, they were silent for a time. It felt like they were changing gears. She said, "Yes," and nodded. We continued going through the things in their home. They were now working together.

EXERCISE

Take a tour of your shared space. Start with one room. Focus on each thing in the room. With each item, ask, "If you were out shopping, would you buy this?" See what each of you feels. Listen to the other person. Don't try to talk them out of their choice. You're just looking and listening. Ask each other, "Do you still like this, or can we let it go?" Take a look at your car and your home itself, and ask, "Would we buy this today?" Make it playful. It helps you be honest. It's interesting to hear what you have to say.

Now, stand together in front of a mirror.

- What do you think of these people?
- What do you think is going on with them?
- What do you see that they don't see?
- What do you like about them?
- Would you like to hang out with them?
- Would you like to be in a relationship like theirs?

Your relationship is as much a thing as the objects in your home. It's easy to get distracted from your relationship and forget its value. But it's good to take a look and ask. This awareness wakes up sleeping parts of us. When we are awake, we can start to take care of our lives.

Taking Care

This work is about taking care of ourselves. We used to think we had to cover up with many layers of protection, whether it was possessions that made us feel powerful or ways of being that made us feel bigger and better. But our experience was that we were left feeling fearful and weaker. As we started losing our reliance on this false armor, we began to experience an uncovered, direct, and sensitive relationship with ourselves. We had a "Where did that come from?" experience as we found ourselves fulfilled in the moment. Our natural presence had a chance to rise to the surface, and we were charmed!

When we open in this way, we experience sharing this powerful feeling of unity with others. We see that it's the clutter in our homes, hearts, and minds that keeps us from enjoying our connections with others. Compassionately removing the clutter piece by piece, together, helps us uncover the radiant jewels in our hearts reflecting their lights off one another.

I encourage you to continue clutter busting and uncovering this living treasure chest!

This morning I
woke up next to
a brand-new day...
and the only
thing I could
do was say hello.

SUMMARY OF PRINCIPLES

- You're letting go of clutter to make room for yourself.

- No object is more important than your peace of mind.

- The greatest experience is unity. No amount of power and control and wealth can surpass that.

- We think, "When I finally get _____, I'll be happy." But happiness is inherent in us. Joy comes to life when we clear out whatever obstructs our connection with our hearts.

- We think that if we control someone they will do what we want, and we'll be happy. But controlling behavior causes resentment, and people suffer.

- After your connection with yourself, your relationships with others are your priority. If a certain relationship isn't a priority, look at whether you need to let it go.

- Clutter busting together requires nonjudgmental awareness, kind encouragement, and openness. Accept and honor the other person's choices, and your relationship will thrive.

ACKNOWLEDGMENTS

I received an unbelievable amount of support while writing this book.

I'm thankful to Julia Mossbridge for her endearing love and encouragement. I'm lucky to have her in my life. I also appreciate her editing assistance with this book.

I'm grateful for the wonderful and supportive people over at New World Library: the editorial director, Georgia Hughes; editors Mimi Kusch and Jeff Campbell; the managing editor, Kristen Cashman; the cover designer, Tracy Cunningham; the production designer, Tona Pearce Myers; the publicity director, Monique Muhlenkamp; and the editorial assistant, Jonathan Wichmann.

I appreciate the support and encouragement of my agent, Katie Boyle, and of my friends Gregory Gardner, Craig Shaynak, Wayne Liquorman, Joseph Mossbridge, Ed Walbridge, Tom Hodges; of my parents, Jon and Lyn Palmer; and of the Carsellos (Sheri, Marina, Celeste, Rob, and Oliver).

I especially want to thank my clients and blog readers, who continue to amaze and inspire me with their courage to take an honest look at their lives and remove the things that are in the way of their happiness.

ABOUT THE AUTHOR

Brooks Palmer is the author of the bestselling *Clutter Busting: Letting Go of What's Holding You Back*, which has been translated into five languages. He has been helping clients clear clutter from their homes, garages, offices, and lives for more than a decade. He also performs stand-up comedy regularly. A member of the Screen Actors Guild, he has appeared in several commercials and films. Palmer divides his time between Chicago and Los Angeles. Visit his clutter-busting website at www.ClutterBusting.com and his humor website at www.BetterLateThanDead.com.

NEW WORLD LIBRARY is dedicated to publishing books and other media that inspire and challenge us to improve the quality of our lives and the world.

We are a socially and environmentally aware company, and we strive to embody the ideals presented in our publications. We recognize that we have an ethical responsibility to our customers, our staff members, and our planet.

We serve our customers by creating the finest publications possible on personal growth, creativity, spirituality, wellness, and other areas of emerging importance. We serve New World Library employees with generous benefits, significant profit sharing, and constant encouragement to pursue their most expansive dreams.

As a member of the Green Press Initiative, we print an increasing number of books with soy-based ink on 100 percent postconsumer-waste recycled paper. Also, we power our offices with solar energy and contribute to nonprofit organizations working to make the world a better place for us all.

Our products are available
in bookstores everywhere.
For our catalog, please contact:

New World Library
14 Pamaron Way
Novato, California 94949

Phone: 415-884-2100 or 800-972-6657
Catalog requests: Ext. 50
Orders: Ext. 52
Fax: 415-884-2199
Email: escort@newworldlibrary.com

To subscribe to our electronic newsletter, visit
www.newworldlibrary.com